Local Government in
NORTH CAROLINA

Gordon P. Whitaker

The University of North Carolina at Chapel Hill

North Carolina City and County
Management Association
Raleigh, North Carolina

 Glencoe

New York, New York   Columbus, Ohio   Chicago, Illinois   Peoria, Illinois   Woodland Hills, California

About the Author

Gordon P. Whitaker is Professor of Public Administration and Government in the School of Government of the University of North Carolina at Chapel Hill. His research interests include citizen participation, local government organization and management, alternative public service delivery arrangements (including nonprofit agencies), civic education, and professional education for public service. In 1997 he helped found the North Carolina Civic Education Consortium, and he serves as its faculty adviser.

Professor Whitaker's research has been supported by grants from the National Science Foundation, the National Institute of Justice, the North Carolina Governor's Crime Commission, and the Jesse Ball du Pont Fund. In 1997 he received the International City/County Management Association's Award for Local Government Education for his work in civic education.

Professor Whitaker has taught at the University of North Carolina at Chapel Hill since 1973. He served from 1980 to 1993 as director of the UNC Master of Public Administration Program. His teaching includes courses in performance evaluation, organization theory, public management and leadership, and state and local government. Before coming to UNC, he was on the faculty of Brooklyn College/City University of New York. Professor Whitaker received his Ph.D. in Political Science from Indiana University in 1972.

Glencoe

The McGraw·Hill Companies

Send all inquires to:
Glencoe/McGraw-Hill
8787 Orion Place
Columbus, OH 43240

ISBN 0-07-831433-X

Printed in the United States of America

1 2 3 4 5 6 7 8 9 10   009   08 07 06 05 04 03 02

Contents

To The Teacher

This book will help students understand how local government in North Carolina works. Students will be able to see how they are affected every day by local government. They will learn that they can play an active role in their own communities and be personally involved in maintaining an effective government.

Each chapter in this book includes definitions of **key terms** in the margins for quick reference, **articles from local newspapers,** and **discussion questions.** The newspaper articles relay current events and help students understand the relevance of certain aspects of local government. Use the discussion questions at the end of each chapter to involve your students in a conversation about how government works around them. Students may answer the questions on a separate sheet of paper in small groups or simply discuss them as a class.

Encourage students to talk about what they learn with friends and family, and to ask questions of government employees or volunteers in their community. This book is designed to help students understand the many facets of local government and see how people working together make a difference. By studying this material, they will appreciate what local government does for them and what they can also do to participate in their government.

Photo Credits

We in North Carolina are a little spoiled when it comes to local government. We have a long tradition of responsible management of our cities and counties, which may explain why a large percentage of the public seems to take their local government for granted. Other than the annual challenge of adopting a balanced budget and the occasional hotly debated new project seeking appropriate zoning or use permits, local government issues rarely grab the spotlight. But local government touches our lives every day.

It is local government that supplies water to our faucets, collects our trash, moves traffic through our downtowns, and cuts the grass in our parks and ball fields. It is also local government that delivers care and counseling to those facing difficult times and responds with qualified personnel to life's emergencies. Our cities and counties provide critical services, but they do it without a lot of fanfare.

The members of the North Carolina City and County Management Association are proud to work for local elected officials in delivering services to the public. We believe that we have one of the most rewarding jobs in the world, managing departments that reach thousands of people every day. We take great pride, too, in our workforce—local government employees using their education and skills for the benefit of the community.

Those of us who make careers in local government are committed to public service. We understand that much of the work we do is behind the scenes and taken for granted. There are times, however, when cities and counties need to hear from the public. For instance, elected officials want to hear from all affected parties when they are considering adding or eliminating programs, formulating a plan to recover from the loss of a major community employer, or deciding on capital projects to be funded by a bond referendum. Managers and department heads want to hear from the public about community problems—such as malfunctioning traffic lights, neglected or abandoned buildings, and animals that are being mistreated—as well as suggestions for improving everyday services. Elected officials and staff are constantly seeking input from the "customers" of local government, but have become accustomed to hearing from only a few voices. Tools such as cable broadcasting of board meetings, citizen surveys, Web sites offering detailed information and direct access to local government officials, and the creation of public affairs offices are all attempts to open those lines of communication.

Our association's Civic Education Project is another approach to fostering involvement in local government. In 1989 our membership became aware that teachers had few if any materials about local government to share with their students. We pledged to fill that gap so students could learn about local government as they learn about federal and state government. At our request, Gordon P. Whitaker, now Professor of Government at the Institute of Government at the University of North Carolina at Chapel Hill, volunteered many hours to researching and writing the first edition of this text. Funding from a variety of sources, including individual cities and counties, made the textbook available free of charge to public high school classrooms in 1993. With the hiring of part-time Civic Education Coordinator Jan Boyette a year later, we began issuing an annual newsletter publicizing the textbook and teacher's guide and directing teachers to other resources available through their own city and county governments. Next, we recruited Wake County elementary teachers Margaret C. Henderson and Laura Mills Clougherty to design lesson plans based on the text for third and fourth grade teachers. In 1998 came a Web site for teachers (www.ncmanagers.org/teachers) and a package of tips and activities for local government officials invited into the classroom. That same year, the association became a founding partner in the North Carolina Civic Education Consortium, a statewide umbrella organization for groups working from many different perspectives to encourage community involvement by young people. The textbook was first made available on the Web site in 1999. The following year, we provided research assistance to Dr. Whitaker to begin work on this updated, second edition of the text. By 2001 we had begun offering an intensive, two-and-a-half day seminar for teachers to demonstrate hands-on learning activities about local government.

It has been my distinct honor to lead the association's Civic Education Committee for the past three years as we have worked to share our enthusiasm for local government with North Carolina's teachers and students. It is our hope that today's students will gain a solid understanding of the functions of city and county government in North Carolina and become active, involved citizens in their communities. And if some of those students should choose to become local government staff members or elected officials, we will be pleased to have a played a part in sparking that commitment to public service.

W. Brian Hiatt

Brian Hiatt
Chair, Civic Education Committee
North Carolina City and County Management Association
City Manager, City of Concord

Acknowledgments

The updated version of this book was made possible through the financial support of the North Carolina City and County Management Association. I thank the members of NCCCMA and especially Brian Hiatt, City Manager of Concord and chair of the NCCCMA Civic Education Committee, for their continuing enthusiastic support of this project.

Jan Boyette, NCCCMA's Civic Education Coordinator, has been responsible for coordinating all the administrative and technical arrangements for making the book available on the Web. Erin Norfleet, my Master of Public Administration (MPA) research assistant on the updated version, located supplementary materials and helped make the book more lively and enjoyable.

Many people helped me write this book. Their contributions have made it more accurate, more interesting, and easier to read. In the listing that follows, I indicate people's affiliations at the time I drafted the book.

My original research assistants on this project—MPA students Hana Kohn, Tim Leshan, Marcy Onieal, Eric C. Peterson, and Roger Schlegel—located materials and provided many useful ideas and suggestions on various versions of the manuscript. The MPA office staff, Jean Coble and Kathy Frymoyer, helped me coordinate the original project with NCCCMA. I thank them for attending to the details of project administration.

I also thank my faculty colleagues for their careful review of the manuscript. Dr. Carolyn Grubbs of Meredith College, Dr. Nanette Mengel of the University of North Carolina at Chapel Hill MPA Program, and Professors David Lawrence and Warren J. Wicker of the UNC Institute of Government each gave me valuable suggestions.

Several high school teachers also took time to read earlier versions of the book. I appreciate greatly the help of James T. Coble, Hickory High School, Hickory; Judy Daniels, Hoggard High School, Wilmington; Pat Gurley, Mt. Olive Junior High School, Mt. Olive; Ann Heafner, West Lincoln High School, Lincolnton; Vennie James, Smithfield-Selma High School, Smithfield; Ricky McDevitt, Madison High School, Marshall; Marcie Pachino, Jordan High School, Durham; Peggy Shonosky, Laney High School, Wilmington; and Darnell Tabron, Jordan High School, Durham. Doug Robertson and John Ellington of the NC State Department of Public Instruction provided valuable assistance.

Local government leaders have also contributed. The members of the NCCCMA Civic Education Committee and Reading Committee provided valuable direction for the project. City council members and county commissioners all across the state voted to pay to make this book available to the state's public school students. Many local government professionals also shared their comments on the manuscript. My special thanks go to Raymond Boutwell, Wake County; Margot Christensen, NC League of Municipalities; Debra Henzey, NC Association of County Commissioners; James Hipp, Lenoir; J. Thomas Lundy, Catawba County; R. Lee Matthews, Hamlet; J. Michael Moore, Thomasville; Robert Shepherd, Land-of-Sky Regional Council; Robert Shepherd, Jr., Kernersville; Kenneth Windley, Davie County; and John Witherspoon, Cabarrus County.

Most especially, I thank Carolyn Carter, Bob Slade and Brian Hiatt, who each chaired the NCCCMA Civic Education Committee, for their encouragement and support. They provided the leadership that directed and sustained this project.

Gordon P. Whitaker

Gordon P. Whitaker
Chapel Hill

Sponsors

Civic Education Project Sponsors at Time of Publication

The North Carolina City and County Management Association gratefully acknowledges the support of the following jurisdictions. These counties and municipalities already have contributed to the association's five-year fundraising campaign to continue the work of the Civic Education Project. Those listed in bold type have made contributions covering their entire commitment for FY 2001–2002 through FY 2005–2006.

Local Government Champions

(Jurisdictions contributing double the requested amount)

Bertie County	Sampson County	Town of Kernersville	Town of Tarboro
Cabarrus County	Town of Angier	City of Laurinburg	Town of Waynesville
Currituck County	Town of Canton	Town of Lewisville	
Dare County	**City of Concord**	Town of Norwood	
Macon County	Town of Harrisburg	City of Rocky Mount	

Local Government Sponsors

Anson County	Town of Bogue	City of Havelock	Town of Pembroke
Carteret County	**City of Brevard**	**City of Hendersonville**	Town of Pollocksville
Catawba County	Town of Bryson City	City of Hickory	**City of Raleigh**
Cherokee County	**City of Burlington**	Town of Hillsborough	Town of Ramseur
Chowan County	Town of Candor	Town of Holly Ridge	Town of Red Springs
Cleveland County	Town of Cape Carteret	Town of Holly Springs	Town of Richlands
Craven County	Town of Carolina	Town of Hudson	Town of Rolesville
Duplin County	Beach	Town of Jackson	**Town of Rutherford**
Franklin County	**Town of Cary**	Town of Jamestown	**College**
Granville County	Town of Cerro Gordo	**Town of Kill Devil**	City of Salisbury
Hertford County	Town of Chapel Hill	**Hills**	Town of Sandyfield
Johnston County	City of Charlotte	City of Kinston	City of Sanford
Jones County	**Village of Clemmons**	Town of Kure Beach	Town of Sedalia
Lincoln County	Town of Conetoe	**City of Lincolnton**	**Town of Smithfield**
McDowell County	**Town of Davidson**	**Town of Linden**	Town of Southern Pines
Nash County	Town of Dortches	City of Lumberton	Town of Southern
Pamlico County	Town of Drexel	Town of Macclesfield	Shores
Person County	City of Dunn	Town of Manteo	Town of Taylorsville
Pitt County	Town of Edenton	City of Marion	Town of Wade
Randolph County	Town of Emerald Isle	Town of Matthews	**Town of Wadesboro**
Swain County	Town of Erwin	City of Mineral Springs	City of Washington
Vance County	**Town of Falcon**	Town of Minnesott	Town of Weaverville
Washington County	Village of Flat Rock	Beach	Town of Webster
Town of Aberdeen	Village of Foxfire	Town of Mocksville	**Town of Wendell**
Town of Ahoskie	Village	City of Monroe	Town of White Lake
City of Albemarle	**Town of Fuqay-Varina**	**Town of Mooresville**	Town of Williamston
Village of Bald Head	**Town of Garner**	City of Mount Airy	City of Wilmington
Island	Town of Gibson	**Town of Murphy**	Town of Windsor
City of Belmont	City of Graham	Town of Nags Head	Town of Winfall
Town of Benson	**Town of Granite Falls**	City of New Bern	City of Winston-Salem
City of Bessemer City	Town of Greenevers	City of Newton	Town of Youngsville
Town of Black	**Town of Hamilton**	City of Northwest	
Mountain	Town of Harrells	Town of Oak Ridge	

Local Government and You

1

Local governments affect our lives in many ways. They supply the water we drink. They provide police and fire protection. They operate the public schools, parks, and libraries. They help people in need. They regulate how land is used and enforce state and local laws. They work to bring new jobs to our communities. Local governments are important to you because they help determine how well you and your neighbors live.

In this book, you will learn about local governments (cities, towns, and counties) in North Carolina. You will explore the ways that local government affects people and the ways that people can influence their local government. You will examine how local governments are organized and the ways they operate. Lastly, you will be introduced to some of the people who make local government work.

Purposes of Local Government

The purpose of local government is to make life better for the people in the community. Local governments try to do this in three ways.

First, local governments provide services. Water supply, fire protection, schools, parks, and libraries are among the many services they provide. Most people use some of these services every day. There are also services that help people with special needs or help people in times of crisis.

Second, local governments encourage community improvement. They do so by encouraging new businesses, sponsoring community festivals and clean-up days, and organizing human relations commissions.

Third, local governments protect people from harmful things. Making and enforcing laws to protect the public are important local government responsibilities. Although the state government in

This high school in Camden County is an example of a service that local governments provide.

Local governments sponsor public events to enrich community life.

federal system:
the sharing of power between the central and state governments

jurisdiction:
the right to use legal authority or the territory over which a government can use its authority

municipality:
a city, town, or village that has an organized government with authority to make laws, provide services, and collect and spend taxes and other public funds

North Carolina makes most of the criminal laws, local law enforcement agencies investigate most of the crimes and make most of the arrests. Crime is not the only kind of harmful behavior. People may also harm others without intending to do so. Local governments set regulations to prevent this. For example, local governments might restrict factories from locating next to houses or they might regulate where and when people park their cars.

National, State, and Local Governments

Often when people speak about "the government," they mean the United States government, but we have several types of governments in this country. We have a **federal system** of government. National, state, and local governments each have their areas of responsibility and authority. The national government in Washington, D.C., is responsible for dealing with problems that affect the entire country. We often call our national government the federal government because it is made up of states. North Carolina is one of 50 states that make up the United States of America. Each state government is responsible for problems within its **jurisdiction.** Each state has also established local governments to deal with the particular "close to home" needs of the people.

Each government has the responsibility to serve the best interests of all the people, the authority to make and enforce laws and to provide services, and the authority to tax to raise funds to support its work.

Each citizen of the United States is also a citizen of the state in which he or she lives. Citizens of North Carolina are also citizens of the county in which they live. People who live within city or town limits are also citizens of that **municipality.** Each level of government—federal, state, county, and municipal—is governed by elected officials. Each level of government provides certain services, regulates certain kinds of activity, and undertakes programs to improve public well-being.

The national government makes laws and carries out policies that affect the entire country. The United States Constitution, for example, applies to all residents of the United States and to all governments in the United States. State and local governments may not pass or enforce laws that contradict the Constitution. For example, the Constitution requires that state and local governments provide "equal protection under the law" to all people.

Among the services operated by the federal government are mail delivery; Social Security benefit payments; and recreation opportunities in national parks, forests, and recreation areas. The national government regulates activities such as the manufacture and sale of medicines, the sale of stocks and bonds, and the operation of nuclear electrical generating plants. National government

The United States; North Carolina; Union County

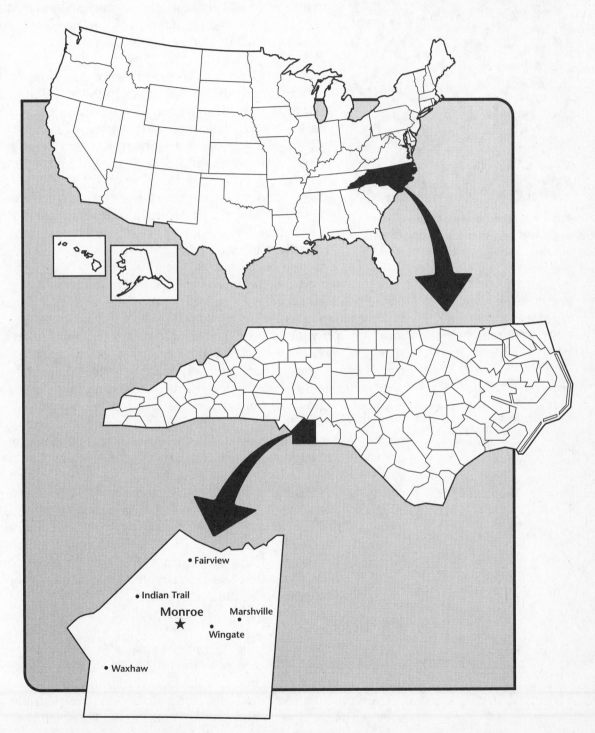

Fairview

Indian Trail

Monroe ★

Marshville

Wingate

Waxhaw

Each citizen of the United States is also a citizen of the state and county where he or she lives.

Police and other local government employees help keep the community safe.

programs for the general well-being of the populace include defense, research, and transportation. The Army, Navy, and Air Force provide national defense. The National Science Foundation, the National Institutes of Health, and other agencies support studies of diseases and possible cures. Federal grants support highway and airport construction.

The North Carolina state government also provides many services. It is responsible for building, maintaining, and policing the state's highways. State government provides recreation opportunities in state parks, forests, and recreation areas. It helps people locate jobs and provides unemployment benefits to those who are unemployed. The state government regulates such matters as insurance rates, waste disposal, and development along the North Carolina coast. Among the state's programs to improve the general well-being of its populace are the recruitment of industry to the state, agricultural research, and promotion of the arts.

mandate:
a legal order by which one government requires actions by another government

grant:
money given by state or federal government to local governments to fund local projects

In the chapters that follow, we will see that federal and state governments influence local governments. One sort of influence involves **mandates** by which federal or state governments require local governments to provide a service or to carry out services in specified ways. Mandates say how counties should operate programs of assistance like Medicaid and food stamps. Federal and state governments also provide **grants** to help fund some local government programs like police services or housing repairs.

Federal and state governments greatly influence some local governments through their decisions about the location and operation of facilities like hospitals, prisons, parks and forests, and military bases. Closing a hospital or military base, expanding a prison, or changing policies on timber harvest or tourism on state or federal land often has a major impact on the local economy. Therefore, the local government in whose jurisdiction those facilities are located is directly affected by these decisions. In North Carolina, local governments can do only things the state government gives them authority to do. Thus, the state can also prevent local governments from doing things opposed to state policy.

Local governments focus on local issues. Like other governments, they provide services, make and enforce laws, and collect taxes to support their work. Local governments also have the responsibility to serve and protect everyone in their jurisdiction. They also often undertake programs to improve the local community.

Everyone in a local government's jurisdiction is responsible for obeying its local laws and paying local taxes. This includes not only the residents of the jurisdiction but also people who work, shop, or visit there, and people who own property there. Everyone, regardless of place of residence, has the right to be treated fairly by local government officials of every local jurisdiction in the United States.

Often there is considerable overlap between local issues and broader interests. One town's use of a river to carry away its wastewater can interfere with the use of that same river as a source of drinking water by towns downstream. Local governments often work closely together to deal with such problems. Most local governments in North Carolina participate in one of the 17 **regional councils** in the state. Local governments join together in the Council of Governments in their area. They pay dues to support the work of the regional council and appoint representatives to meet to discuss problems they share and to work out ways to deal with those problems.

Local governments also cooperate directly with each other. They usually have **mutual aid agreements** to help each other fight fires or deal with other emergencies. Often a county and the municipalities within it work together in various ways, including building libraries or parks, setting up recycling or economic development programs, planning and controlling land use, and collecting taxes.

regional council:
an organization of local governments established to deal with mutual challenges; 17 exist in North Carolina

mutual aid agreement:
commitments by local governments to assist each other in times of need

People and Local Government

You and the other residents make up the population of your county, city, or town. Together you make up the community that your local government represents. You are the people who most regularly use the services of your local government. Its laws and its community improvement activities affect you. If you have lived in your community for some time, you probably identify yourself with your local government and feel some pride in it.

Any group of people who share common bonds can be thought of as a community. You may also think of yourself as belonging to other communities—a neighborhood or an ethnic or religious group, for example. However, these informal communities do not have governmental authority or responsibility. They play a very different part in your life than do local governments. Local governments have the authority and the responsibility to regulate what people do and also the authority to make people pay to support and protect the community.

It is often difficult to decide how best to meet the needs of all the people in a local government's jurisdiction. People may disagree about whether they need another swimming pool or new tennis courts, about where to locate a landfill or sewage treatment plant, or about the need for sponsoring a teen center. They may disagree about the need to increase local taxes to pay for public services.

Elected officials have the difficult responsibility of deciding what the needs of the community are and what the government should do. As representatives of the people, they have the authority for

In the NEWS...

Making It Easier to Come to the Aid of Neighboring Local Governments

By Eleanore J. Hajian

Tarboro Town Manager Sam Noble can quickly sum up his situation following Hurricane Floyd: no power, no water, no wastewater treatment, no roads and limited food.

"It was pretty scary," he said. "You've just got to improvise and persevere."

Noble knew what to do about the power. As a longtime manager of a town in the electric distribution business, he had done it many times before. He had to call the regional emergency coordinator for Electri-Cities (an association providing technical, emergency and other services to its members) who would find and send help.

Getting help with other needs—starting up the water plant, locating heavy equipment, finding police officers and building inspectors—wasn't so simple. Neighboring municipalities couldn't help because they were also under water, and state emergency resources were stretched thin because of the magnitude of the disaster. So Noble did what all people do when they need help—he called his friends, the city and county managers he knew best from other parts of the state. At the same time, they called him.

"I'm very fortunate because I've gotten to know a lot of people and almost all of them were concerned and called or e-mailed me to ask if they could help."

Ultimately, Noble found and received the help he needed. He also spent a lot of time and energy getting it.

Scrambling to find emergency assistance is a reality managers across the state have faced. Each county in the state has felt the wrath of at least one of the 14 presidentially declared disasters to hit North Carolina. They

Flooded roads are sometimes not the only obstacle to getting aid to other municipalities when natural disasters strike.

include eight hurricanes, four winter storms, one flood and one tornado, according to state emergency management officials.

But what if Noble had an emergency assistance coordinator to call for municipal help like he did for the city's electric service?

"If there were one person to call and say, 'I need five dump trucks and 10 police officers,' and everyone knew to call that one person to offer assistance, it would be much better," he said. "It's great to have people call you directly to offer assistance, but it's really hard to call all those people back when you're up to your [ears] in alligators."

Next time, that's all Noble will have to do, if everything goes according to plan.

A new mutual aid coordinator established through the League and the N.C. Association of County Commissioners will serve local governments seeking and offering assistance to each other in disasters when the State Emergency Response Team (SERT) is activated. Paid volunteers from cities, towns, and counties will serve as mutual aid coordinators.

(Continued from page 6)

It is the first time local governments will have one of their own acting as a full member of SERT.

Previously, SERT, which is assembled in response to, or in preparation for a disaster, was made up of core emergency responders representing several state agencies, as well as the National Guard, ElectriCities, private utility operators and private relief organizations such as the American Red Cross.

But experience with Hurricane Fran and then Hurricane Floyd made the need for local government representation apparent, said John Spurrell, NCLM Environmental Policy Analyst.

"Local governments play an integral role in responding to emergencies and assisting neighbors during disasters, and in the wake of Hurricane Floyd it became prudent to have a local government representative on SERT to help coordinate local assistance from one point, rather than to depend upon many informal arrangements," Spurrell said.

—Excerpted with permission from *Southern City*, August 2000.

deciding the policies and programs of local governments. Elected officials select local government employees (either directly or indirectly) and oversee their work. In later chapters we will explore the specific responsibilities of various elected officials.

Local government employees carry out the work of local government. They make sure that safe drinking water is readily available. They answer calls for police assistance, fight fires, maintain public buildings, and help those who need public assistance. Local government employees include lifeguards at the public swimming pool, your public librarian, and the city or county manager. Public employees are responsible for putting local government policies and programs into practice. You will learn more about their work in later chapters.

All those who live, work, own property, or otherwise have an interest in a community have the right to request public services from the local government and to let local government officials know about their concerns. There are several ways to share concerns. Citizens can call city, town, or county offices; talk to local elected officials; write letters to the local newspaper; or attend public meetings.

People in a community can learn about local public issues by reading the newspaper and by talking to friends. In more and more communities, local public-affairs television programs and local government Web pages are available. Citizens can expand their knowledge of public issues and programs by reading materials from the library and by discussing the issues with local government officials.

County commissioners often struggle to finance local services like public schools while dealing with more state mandates and less state funding.

In the
NEWS...
Painting a True Picture of Crime

By Eleanore J. Hajian

The 12 residents listened intently as the police officer gave a report on crime occurring in their Raleigh neighborhood. On this day, the officer had good news. "Nothing really serious has been reported here in a while," Officer W.L. Norvell reassured.

At one time, reports of drug dealing and the violent crimes associated with it would have filled the officer's roster. But long-term residents, many of whom are senior citizens, got fed up with being scared and started a community watch group that regularly draws crowds of 30 or more people.

"I got tired of the crime and other people did too," said the group's chair Mildred Flynn.

Today, the neighborhood's situation has drastically improved, Flynn said. But the regular meetings still remain vital to keeping residents informed, and keeping crime at bay. It helps to know what's really happening in your neighborhood and where, Flynn said. That way, with the help of police officers, residents can figure out what to do about it.

Giving residents an accurate portrayal of crime in their neighborhood is a key component of crime prevention, said Officer Lisa Weber-Brglez, who has worked a lot with the group in her job as a crime prevention and community education officer with the Raleigh Police Department.

With reports of kidnappings, murders, car jackings, bank robberies and school shootings filling headlines, people's perceptions of

A police officer reviews crime data to help prevent crimes in the future.

crime and what crime is actually occurring can be very different things. Those perceptions alter the way people live, and the steps they take to protect themselves from crime, say law enforcement authorities. Wrong perceptions can cause inappropriate reactions ranging from exaggerated fears to perilous complacency.

As part of their crime prevention programs, police departments across the state have turned to community outreach programs and assigned officers like Weber-Brglez to set the record straight.

Since 1995, the department has reached out to the community by establishing substations throughout the city, encouraging officers to talk to residents on their beats, dedicating personnel to domestic violence cases and working with a court-oriented victims' assistance program.

—Excerpted with permission from *Southern City,*
February 2000.

Voters in local government jurisdictions have a great impact on local government decisions. Voters can affect decisions indirectly by voting for officials who reflect the voters' views and directly by voting in local **referendums.** In addition to voting, citizens can affect local government decisions by running for and being elected to public office or by voicing their concerns to local government officials.

referendum:
a way for citizens to vote on state or local laws

Hurricane Floyd Operations in the City of Rocky Mount

City Departments	County and Regional Agencies and Affiliates
Fire Department	Edgecombe County Emergency Services
Police Department	Nash County Emergency Services
Utilities Department	Battleboro Volunteer Fire Department
Water Resources Department	Bay Leaf Rescue Squad
Public Works Department	Coats Grove Swift Water Rescue Team
Engineering Department	Harnett County Water Rescue Team
Planning and Community Development Department	North Central Underwater Recovery Team
Parks and Recreation Department	Stokes County Mountain Rescue Team
City Clerk	Stoney Creek Rescue Squad
Finance Department	West Edgecombe Rescue Squad
Human Relations Department	West Edgecombe Volunteer Fire Department
Human Resources Department	Human Society Rescue Squad

Mutual Aid From Within North Carolina	State Cooperating Agencies
City of Greensboro	North Carolina National Guard
City of Henderson	North Carolina Division of Community Correction
City of High Point	
City of Lexington	
City of Morganton	
Town of Nashville	
City of Raleigh	
City of Sanford	
Wake County	
Town of Wrightsville Beach	

Assistance From Outside North Carolina	Federal Assistance
City of Marietta, Georgia	U.S. Army, 318th Aviation Wing (Fort Bragg)
City of Newnam, Georgia	U.S. Army Reserve
Pennsylvania Task Force One	

Learning About Local Government

When you need public services, where can you get them? How can local governments help you resolve public disputes? What are your responsibilities as a citizen of local government? How can you participate in making your community a better place to live?

Because local governments affect your life in so many ways and because they should be open to your participation and influence, you need to know about your local government. In the chapters

In the
NEWS...

Special Parks Add Spice to the Recreational Flavor in Tar Heel Communities

By Eleanore Hajian and Tara Humphries

Most people have to go to an airport to see things fly, but in Chapel Hill people can go to Ryan's World.

Few days go by without a young man catapulting himself through the air at the ultra-cool skateboard park. One by one they dive off the ramps, jump over hills and slide down rails. General technique: ignore the law of gravity. (And just in case this technique fails, wear knee pads and helmets.)

After years of planning, controversy, petitioning and negotiating for insurance coverage, the town council decided in 1995 to make the park a reality by allocating $50,000 to the project. The council made the move after years of petitioning by skateboarding fans who wanted a place in town to skate legally. Chapel Hill is among at least nine towns and cities that have made the same decision. Skateboard parks are a trend that has caught on, said Sharon Tebbutt, a consultant with the N.C. State Recreation Resources Service. "Skateboarding is super hot right now," she said. "A lot of teens are into it and they are speaking out and so are their parents."

Since opening in November [1999], skateboarders from all over the Triangle have kept it busy, said Frank Noel, concessionaire and operator for Chapel Hill's park.

"It's been a steady business," he said. "Skateboarding is a sport and it's a very popular sport. In two years we expect it to become an Olympic sport."

Most of the park's customers are ages 16 and under, but several highly talented 20-somethings also frequent Ryan's World. Despite the focus on younger teens, the park has already become nationally known among skateboarders.

After covering the $75,000 construction of the park, Chapel Hill contracted with Noel to run the park as a business, said Kathryn Spatz, recreation director. The town receives a share of the profit.

To skate, town residents pay a $5 annual membership fee and then $5 for all day skating privileges. Non-members pay $7 for a day of skating. Non-resident fees are a dollar higher. The park is open every day except Monday. Eventually the 40-acre property where the skateboard park is located will be a multi-activity complex for the whole family, Spatz said. The town has plans to build a batting cage, two softball fields and possibly an aquatic fun park.

—Excerpted with permission from *Southern City*, June 2000.

Teens helped convince town officials to build a skateboard park.

that follow, you will read about how North Carolina's cities, towns, and counties provide public services, how they protect the public from harmful activities, and how they improve the community you live in.

This book includes interviews with some of the people who make local governments work. It also includes excerpts from newspaper stories about local government. The interviews and stories are examples of the kinds of information you can collect about local governments in your own part of the state.

Some of the terms used to discuss government may be new to you. The words in bold are defined in the margins for a quick reference and are also in the Glossary. If you encounter a word that is unfamiliar, first check the Glossary. If it is not included there, look for the word in a dictionary.

Discussion questions at the end of each chapter are a further guide for applying what you learn from this book to your own city, town, or county. There is a list of books and magazines concerning the topics discussed in this book under "For Further Reading." Many of these books and magazines should be in your school library or in the local public library.

Is your school board considering year-round classes? Is the board of county commissioners considering areas for a new landfill? Is the city council debating what to do about noise complaints? As you watch the news on television, read the newspaper, or hear discussions about local government, you will notice issues that affect you. This book can help you understand the ways local governments make decisions about those issues and your responsibilities and opportunities for participating in local government.

Discussion Questions

1. In which local governments' jurisdictions do you live?

2. What services do local governments provide for you and your family?

3. Reread the news story on page 10 about the skateboard park in Chapel Hill. What part did young people in Chapel Hill play in getting the town to build the new park?

4. Local governments have many programs to improve the community. Identify such a program of your local government.

   Which government is involved?

   What activities does the program involve?

   How are these activities supposed to improve the community?

   Is anyone opposed to these activities?

   If so, why are they opposed?

5. The chart on page 9 lists public agencies involved in rescue and recovery efforts in the City of Rocky Mount following Hurricane Floyd, which hit eastern North Carolina in September 1999. (This summary does not attempt to list all the private businesses, churches, and individuals who contributed their time, talents, and financial resources.) What do you think each agency might have done to help deal with the flooding of Hurricane Floyd and the resulting damage to public and private property?

North Carolina Municipalities

People live near one another for many reasons: to conduct business, to live near their workplaces, and to enjoy the company of others, for example. There are many advantages to living in cities and towns, but there are also disadvantages that create issues—issues that affect the community at large.

One such issue is water supply. When houses are close together, individual wells for each house are likely to become contaminated unless there is a public sewer system or other provision for safe disposal of wastes. Moreover, private wells may not provide enough water for fighting fires. Fire threatens an entire community when houses are close enough that fire can easily spread from one house to another. Similarly, noise becomes an issue when people live close enough together to be bothered by the sounds others make.

Municipal governments have been established so that the people living in each place can deal with issues they face as a community. In North Carolina, municipal governments are called cities, towns, or (in a few cases) villages. In North Carolina, these terms carry no special legal meaning. All three terms refer to a municipality created by the state that is authorized to make decisions for a community and to carry out the policies and programs that have been approved. (In common usage, "towns" are often thought of as smaller than "cities," but this is not always true. The Town of Cary, for example, is now the seventh largest municipality in North Carolina. It had more than 94,000 residents in 2000.) North Carolina law establishes the powers and responsibilities of each municipality.

These houses in Wilmington were built when Wilmington was North Carolina's largest city. Like most houses in cities and towns, they were built close together.

The Development of Towns and Cities in North Carolina

European settlers established the first municipal governments in North Carolina in the early 1700s. Although they encountered Native American villages and sometimes built their own towns on the same sites, the Europeans established municipal governments based on English models. Each town was an independent municipality authorized under English, and later North Carolina, law.

Early North Carolina towns maintained public wells, established volunteer fire departments, and set up town watches to keep the peace. For example, the commissioners of Newbern (as it was then spelled) detailed the duties of the town watch in 1794 as follows:

Around 1880, the Eagle Hotel in Asheville welcomed travelers who arrived by stagecoach.

> **"** *The gentlemen on watch are to use their best endeavors to prevent house breaking, and thieving, of every kind, and to seize and secure every person found committing, or attempting to commit any such offenses . . .*
>
> *The watch will take up all suspicious and disorderly persons, who may be found in or strolling about the streets, after nine o'clock at night . . .*
>
> *On discovering any danger by fire, one of the watch will immediately ring the church bell, one other of them will then inform the person, who has care of the water engine, and the others are to alarm the persons near where the greatest danger appears, and use their utmost endeavors, to assist those in distress.* **"**

By 1800 there were more than a dozen municipalities in North Carolina, but only four—Edenton, Fayetteville, New Bern, and Wilmington—had populations of 1,000 or more. North Carolina was a rural, agricultural state, and few people lived in cities or towns. The state remained largely rural throughout the nineteenth century. In 1850, Wilmington, the state's major port, was the only municipality in the state with more than 5,000 residents. Wilmington's population reached 10,000 in 1870. Asheville, Charlotte, and Raleigh each had more than 10,000 residents by 1880.

In the mid-nineteenth century, the North Carolina General Assembly (the state legislature) revised the laws regarding municipalities. Under an act passed in 1855, all municipalities were given the same powers. They could tax real estate; liquor dealers; tickets to shows; dogs; and freely roaming hogs, horses, and cattle. They could appoint a town constable, regulate public markets, prevent public nuisances, protect public health, keep streets and bridges in

Water supply to Raleigh residents improved following construction of this water tower in 1887.

repair, and regulate the quality and weight of loaves of bread baked for sale. As time passed, the General Assembly gave additional authority to individual municipalities and groups of municipalities. As a result, each North Carolina city or town may now have a somewhat different set of powers and responsibilities.

Population growth brought the need for new municipal powers and responsibilities. More people created new problems for municipal governments. For example, adequate supplies of safe drinking water became a problem as cities became larger and more densely populated. The General Assembly established the State Board of Health in 1877. One of its initial concerns was the threat of waterborne diseases in the state's cities and towns. Intestinal diseases like typhoid are caused by bacteria that live in water. The diseases are spread by water that has been contaminated with human wastes.

To help prevent disease, Asheville built a system to supply filtered water to its residents in 1884. Water from the Swannanoa River was pumped four miles from the filtration plant to the city. The year after it was built, the State Board of Health reported that Asheville's new municipal water supply was the safest in the state and that there had been "a marked decrease in typhoid" in Asheville.

Not everyone in Asheville benefited from the new system, however. Although the city owned and operated the water-supply system, it charged 25 cents per thousand gallons of water. This was expensive for workers who supported their families on an average income of about $750 per year. Asheville city water was, therefore, "not in general use among the poorer classes," according to the Board of Health report.

In fact, Asheville's water rates were lower than those in many other cities. Unlike Asheville, most North Carolina city governments did not operate water systems. Instead private companies supplied water to city residents. In Charlotte, the private water company charged 50 cents per thousand gallons, and in Raleigh, the water company charged 40 cents per thousand gallons. Many people could not afford to buy water at these rates. They continued to rely on unsanitary sources of water. Water supply, like many other services, did not become a municipal responsibility in many cities and towns until the twentieth century.

During the early years of the twentieth century, North Carolina towns and cities grew rapidly. By 1920, 20 percent of the state's 2.5 million people lived in municipalities. More cities and towns paved their streets as automobiles became common. They also set up full-time police and fire departments and adopted building codes to regulate construction and reduce hazards to health and safety. Cities and towns bought private water and sewer companies during this period or started their own systems to make these services more widely available to their residents. A number of cities even started their own electric utilities to bring electricity to their communities.

Urban growth continued throughout the twentieth century. Municipal services continued to expand to meet the needs of the state's growing urban population. By 2000 almost all cities and towns had public water and sewer systems, paved streets, and police and fire protection. Other services such as garbage collection, parks, and recreation programs became increasingly common in municipalities throughout the state.

Fire protection is an important service for growing urban populations.

By 2000 Charlotte had more than 540,000 residents, Raleigh had more than 275,000, Greensboro had more than 220,000, and Durham and Winston-Salem each had over 180,000. Most North Carolina cities and towns continue to be small places, however. As the table below shows, only 62 North Carolina cities and towns had 10,000 residents or more in 2000.

Distribution of Municipalities, 2000

Population of Municipality	Number of Municipalities of This Size	Total Population in Municipalities of This Size
Fewer than 2,500	352	302,191
2,500 to 9,999	126	621,811
10,000 to 49,999	47	964,761
50,000 or more	15	2,165,078
All cities and towns	540	4,053,841

Source: Bureau of the Census. Compiled by the North Carolina State Data Center, Office of State Budget, Planning, and Management.

How Municipalities Are Created

corporation:
a group of persons formed by law to act as a single body

contract:
an agreement made between two or more people or organizations

sue:
to ask a court to act against a person or organization to prevent or pay for damage by that person or organization

liability:
something for which one is obligated according to law

levy:
to impose a tax by law

incorporate:
to receive a state charter, officially recognizing the government of a locality

charter:
the document defining how a city or town is to be governed and giving it legal authority to act as a local government

annexation:
the legal process of extending municipal boundaries and adding territory to a city or town

State government establishes cities and towns as municipal **corporations.** Like private corporations, municipal corporations can own property, form **contracts,** and be **sued.** The owners of a corporation give the responsibility of running the corporation to a board. The board acts on behalf of the owners in deciding what the corporation should do. A municipality's "owners"—the citizens of the jurisdiction—elect a board, which is responsible for running the municipality. Because a municipality is a corporation, a citizen's **liability** for municipal debts is limited to the amount of tax the citizen owes the municipality.

Municipal corporations differ from private corporations in important ways. For one thing, citizens become the "owners" of a municipal corporation simply by living within the municipality's jurisdiction. They do not buy the corporation's stock the way owners of a private, for-profit corporation do. Municipal corporations also have different powers than private corporations. Private corporations can engage in any legal activity they choose. North Carolina municipalities can engage only in those activities for which the General Assembly has given its permission, and the General Assembly may change municipal authority as it wishes. For example, the legislature might remove a city's authority to license taxicabs or to operate swimming pools, and that city could then no longer carry out the activity. At the same time, unlike private corporations, municipal corporations are governments. Therefore, municipal corporations have authority to make and enforce laws and to **levy** taxes.

Cities and towns must be **incorporated** by the General Assembly. The General Assembly may require the approval of the voters of the new municipality, but it does not need to do so. An incorporated place has defined geographic boundaries and an approved **charter,** the rules under which it conducts its business.

A new city or town is generally incorporated after the development of a settlement in the area. Some towns grew up around county courthouses and were then incorporated. Others like Ahoskie, Carrboro, and Durham developed around mills or railway stations. The town of Princeville was incorporated by the General Assembly in 1885, 20 years after it was settled as a freedmen's camp by former slaves at the end of the Civil War. People ask for their town to be incorporated because they want to have a local government. They want public services, a means for providing public order and improving the community, and the right to participate in making local decisions.

The extension of municipal boundaries is called **annexation.** When territory is annexed to a city or town, that territory comes within the municipality's jurisdiction and its residents become part of the town's population. Voters in the annexed territory automatically become eligible to vote in the municipality's elections, and the municipality must provide services to the new

In the NEWS...

Rural Hamlet Out to Stay That Way

By Kristen Collins

The glory days of this Harnett County crossroads ended nearly 70 years ago, when the general stores closed, the mills shut down and the trains stopped running.

Today, about all that is left of those times are a post office, a church and some people who still have a dream for Kipling. They are working to make this old railroad stop a town.

"We can still see what we used to have," explained Dayton Smith, 79, whose grandfather renamed the old Bradley's Story community for his favorite author, Rudyard Kipling. "We want to retain that. If we are organized, we've still got a Kipling."

Every year, a few North Carolina communities seek incorporation. Three others—Duck on the coast, Miller's Creek in Wilkes County and Slanting Bridge in Catawba County—are trying this year.

Rapid growth has created dozens of towns in North Carolina. The legislature has approved more than 50 in the past decade, bringing the total to 542. Incorporation protects residents from annexation by a bigger town and gives them the control over development, but some warn that too many new towns could hurt regionalism and drain state coffers.

In Kipling, which would have 1,150 people and 3.9 square miles of land, townhood is a long shot.

State statutes say 40 percent of the land in a new town should be developed. According to the state, 18 percent of Kipling is developed. That fact earned it the only negative recommendation this year from the legislative commission that oversees incorporations. The legislature has the final say.

The 10 or so Kipling residents who worked for half a year—agonizing over budgets, holding public hearings and delivering impassioned speeches—say Kipling's rural character is what they love about the place. And it's the reason they have not given up. Sen[ator] Oscar Harris, a Democrat from Benson, introduced their incorporation bill last week.

Kipling residents say they don't want to hire employees, provide new services or hand out big tax bills; their proposed tax rate is only 13 cents per $100 of property values. They just want to protect the open spaces and tightly knit neighborhoods that have made Kipling, 25 miles south of Raleigh, a refuge.

"If we don't do something, we'll lose the community," said D.H. Baker, Jr., who runs a museum of American Indian artifacts in a shed outside his house.

—Excerpted with permission from *The News & Observer,* Raleigh, North Carolina, March 29, 2001.

---

residents. Cities and towns may annex territory through an act of the General Assembly, by petition of the owners of the property to be annexed, or by **ordinance.** Annexation by ordinance requires that the territory is adjacent to the municipality and that it has already reached a certain level of urban development. Also, the municipality has to show that it will provide services to the annexed territory.

In addition to following its own charter, each North Carolina municipality must also obey state laws and regulations. Some laws apply to all cities or towns of a certain size. These general laws provide most of the authority for North Carolina municipalities. However, sometimes a city wants to do something not authorized

ordinance:
a law, usually of a city or county

Annexations Could Bring in Thousands of New Residents

By Kenwyn Caranna

The recent annexation of almost 1,000 acres eventually could increase Kernersville's population by more than one-third. Plans for the newly annexed land include a mix of residential, commercial and light industrial uses.

The Ridgewood Group of Greensboro requested the annexation of 922 acres along Teague Road, south of Interstate 40. The site includes the Pine Tree Golf Course.

The group plans to rezone the land and build a light industrial, commercial and residential development there, said Planning Director Jeff Hatling.

The development could add between 2,000 and 3,000 new homes to Kernersville, which has a population of about 15,000, Hatling said.

"At the minimum there will be 4,000 new residents in that area and perhaps as many as 7,000 new residents," Hatling said.

Richard Adkins lives near the newly annexed area at 7653 Watkins Ford Road. He isn't pleased with the prospect of so many new neighbors.

"It's going to ruin it," said Adkins, who rents a home adjacent to several acres of farmland. "It will be just like High Point."

Ridgewood is not the only development planned for the area. When the town annexed the land January 18, it also added 77 acres near NC 66 and Shields Road. That property, known as Stafford Centre, is zoned for commercial development. A motel, restaurant and offices are among the businesses being considered for the area, Hatling said.

These developments are just a taste of what could come to the area east of Union Cross and south of I-40, which is mostly farmland and rural homes.

The relocation of a sewer pump station further south along Abbotts Creek, from Old Salem Road to Watkins Ford Road, means more developers will be able to tap into the town's sewer system. That project—which is tied to the Ridgewood development—will open another 3,000 acres in the southeast county area for potential development, town and county planners said.

"The location of that area is inevitable for development," said Paul Norby, director of the City/County Planning Board. The county wants to keep development clustered in strategic areas and leave much of the acreage undeveloped.

"There's a lot of people down in that area who would like to see that semirural atmosphere preserved," Norby said.

Moving the sewer pump station is important if the area is to grow. It will expand the capacity of the station, and environmental regulations require a sewer system for large-scale housing or commercial projects, Hatling said.

Town planners are working with Forsyth County to come up with a plan for developing the area, which is in the Abbotts Creek Watershed. The watershed supplies Lake Thom-A-Lex, a source of drinking water for Thomasville and Lexington, said town engineer Russell Radford.

Planners are conducting a traffic analysis and looking at floodplain and wetland protection to help determine what development is appropriate, Hatling said.

—Reprinted with permission from *Greensboro News & Record*, January 30, 2001.

local act:
a state law that applies to only one local government

by general law or by its charter. Often in such cases the city asks the General Assembly to approve a **local act.** By custom, the General Assembly approves local acts that are favored by all of the representatives to the General Assembly from the jurisdiction that requests the local act.

Governing Cities and Towns

Each municipality has its own governing board, elected by citizens of the city or town. Like the state legislature, a local governing board represents the people of the jurisdiction and has the authority to act for them. In many North Carolina cities and towns, the governing board is called the council, although "board of commissioners" and "board of aldermen" are also names for municipal governing boards.

Regardless of whether they are called council members, commissioners, or aldermen, the members of the governing board make official decisions for the city. The governing board establishes local tax rates and adopts a budget that indicates how the city will spend its money. The governing board sets policies for municipal services, passes ordinances to regulate behavior, and enters into agreements on behalf of the municipality.

The voters also elect a mayor in most North Carolina cities and towns. In a few places, however, the governing board elects the mayor. The mayor presides over the governing board and is typically the chief spokesperson for the municipality. In some other states, the mayor is also the chief administrator for the municipality, but this is not the case in North Carolina.

Except for some of the smallest towns, North Carolina municipalities hire a professional manager (or administrator) to serve as chief executive. Under the **council-manager plan,** the manager is responsible for carrying out the council's policies and for running city government. The city (or town) manager is responsible for hiring and firing municipal employees, for coordinating their work, for advising the council on policy issues, for proposing a municipal budget, and for reporting to the council on municipal activities. The manager "serves at the pleasure of the council." That means the council can fire the manager whenever a majority of the council members decide they want a new manager. A manager must work closely with the council in developing policies for the city and with city employees in seeing that city policies are carried out.

Each municipality also has a clerk. In some cities and towns, the manager appoints the clerk. In others, the council appoints the clerk. Regardless of who makes the appointment, the municipal clerk reports directly to the governing board. The clerk keeps official

People sometimes disagree about urban development and annexation.

council-manager plan: an arrangement for local government in which the elected legislature hires a professional executive to direct government activities

The Council-Manager Plan

The council-manager plan was developed in the United States to provide skilled professional administration for city government. In 1913 Hickory was one of the first cities in the entire country to hire a professional manager. Other North Carolina cities and towns soon followed.

Counties experimented with the plan during the 1920s. In 1929 Robeson County was the first in the nation to adopt the plan and keep using it. Durham County followed in 1930.

Today, North Carolina is one of the states that makes the most use of the council-manager plan of local government.

Most city and county managers are college graduates who have specialized education in public management. Many have graduate degrees—usually a Master of Public Administration degree. Most belong to the International City/County Management Association (ICMA). The ICMA provides professional assistance and continuing education for managers. It also has a Code of Ethics, which emphasizes the public service values professional managers follow.

City/county managers are experts in planning and coordinating local government services. Their Code of Ethics calls on them to use their expertise for the entire community and to stay out of local politics, including elections for local officials. Professional managers help the elected board plan programs and services for the jurisdiction and are responsible for day-to-day administration of city government. Final responsibility for deciding on local policies rests with the elected board.

records of the board's meetings and decisions. The clerk may also publish notices, keep other municipal records, conduct research for the governing board, and carry out a wide variety of other duties, as assigned by the board. The clerk is usually a key source of information for citizens about their municipal government.

Many small municipalities do not have a manager. Where there is no manager, the governing board directs administration of the town's business. The board hires and directs town employees and manages the town's affairs together, as a committee, or assigns day-to-day oversight responsibilities for different departments to different board members. In towns that have no manager, the clerk is often a key administrator in the town and may "wear many hats," in effect holding several different jobs.

personnel:
the people who work for a government, company, or other organization

Municipal employees do much of the work of city and town governments. City **personnel** include police officers, firefighters, water treatment plant operators, recreation supervisors, or others who provide services directly to city residents. Their work is supported by other city personnel: accountants, analysts, engineers, lawyers, secretaries, and a variety of other staff. These personnel provide expert advice, train employees, pay bills, prepare reports, and do the many other things it takes to conduct a city's business.

City personnel are organized into departments. Each department specializes in a particular service, such as police work, fire protection, water supply, or recreation. Typically, the city manager selects department heads. They work with the city manager in planning and coordinating the activities of employees in their departments. In many cities, the manager relies on department heads and/or a personnel department to recruit applicants for city

Working for Local Government

Raleigh's Manager Takes Office

By Sarah Lindenfeld

Monday was Russell Allen's first official day as the city's new manager. But he has been working on city business since he took the job last month.

Allen, 48, the former city manager of Rock Hill, SC, said he has gotten to know city department leaders over the phone. And he and Carolyn Carter, an assistant city manger who had served as interim manager, "huddled by phone" and started the process of looking for a new police chief, he said.

Selecting a successor to former Police Chief Mitch Brown is among Allen's first tasks in Raleigh. Allen met Monday morning with Major John Knox, who has been serving as interim chief since Brown's retirement last year and who wants the job permanently.

Major Ralph Strickland also is interested.

Under the city charter, the city manager, attorney and clerk report to the council. The other department heads answer to the manager, who hires them. Several council members have said they want some influence over the selection.

Allen said he plans to talk with city officials, council members and the community about the hire.

Today, Carter is to guide Allen through the regular City Council meeting at 1 P.M., when council members are to cover a 19-page agenda that includes issues such as zoning cases and parade routes.

"My father had a saying that goes something like this: 'Words cannot express, no pen indicate. . .' and then you fill in whatever you want to fill in," Carter said Monday. "I would

fill in: 'the happiness, excitement and enthusiasm I have that he is here. I have 100 percent confidence in his abilities. I have known him over 20 years, and I know him to be a consummate professional and wonderful human being.'"

Allen spent much of Monday meeting city officials, a few council members and reporters sorting through the usual first-day-on-the-job tasks such as learning to use voice mail and signing up for benefits.

In the morning, staffers in the city manager's office presented Allen, a Harley-Davidson motorcycle fan, with a few welcome gifts including a Harley-Davidson wall clock and a "Harley Parking Only" sign. He had already displayed a couple of miniature versions of the motorcycle, including a Harley-Davidson Heritage Softail Classic.

Allen, who ended his 12-year-career in Rock Hill last week, said he will miss the colleagues he left behind. But he looks forward to getting to know the community in Raleigh. He already has a meeting scheduled with a neighborhood association Wednesday night.

"I feel very fortunate to have this opportunity . . ." he said. "It's just a terrific community."

—Excerpted with permission from *The News & Observer*, Raleigh, North Carolina, April 17, 2001.

On his first day on the job, Russell Allen figures out the city's voice mail system. He has personalized his office with a miniature Harley.

jobs, screen job candidates, and hire new employees. Department heads organize and supervise the employees in their departments.

The people who live in a city or town also play an important role in providing municipal services. Volunteers help supervise recreation programs, organize recycling, and even fight fires. Citizen advisory committees, boards, and commissions help city councils and city employees review and plan programs. Individual citizens influence city policies through petitions, public hearings, and conversations with city officials. Residents also help carry out city programs. They sort their trash for recycling. They call police or fire departments to report dangerous situations. Many municipal services cannot be provided effectively without the active cooperation of residents.

Municipal governments help people make their communities better places to live. They provide services to make life safer, healthier, and happier for the people who live there. They offer incentives for improving the appearance and economy of their community. They make and enforce laws to deal with public problems.

Discussion Questions

These questions are about the city or town where you live. If you do not live in a municipality, answer the questions for a nearby city or town. To answer some of these questions, you may need to do some additional research.

1. Why do people move to your city or town?
   Why might they move away?

2. When was your city or town first settled?
   When was it incorporated?
   Why was it established?

3. Assume that the average family in Asheville used 3,000 gallons of city water per week in 1884. How much did they spend on city water each week?
   What percentage of an average family's income of $14 per week was spent for water?
   In 1991 city water in Asheville cost 35 cents per thousand gallons. An average family used 11,000 gallons per week. How much did the average Asheville family spend for water per week in 1991?
   If an average family's income was $420 per week in 1991, how much of their income did they spend on water?
   How much does water cost per thousand gallons in your city? How many gallons does your

family use each week? (Note: Your city's water rate may be based on cubic feet of water, rather than gallons. There are 231 cubic inches per gallon, about .134 cubic feet per gallon.)

4. What is your municipal governing board called?
   How many seats does it have?

5. Does your city or town use the council-manager plan of government?
   If so, who is the manager (or "administrator")?

6. How many personnel does your city or town have?
   How many departments are there?
   What is the largest department of your municipal government?

7. How have you or someone you know helped your city provide services or improve the community?

8. How does your city or town cooperate with other municipalities?
   With county government?

3 North Carolina Counties

No matter where you live in North Carolina, you live in a county and have a county government. Unlike municipalities, counties were not established to deal with the specific problems of living close together. Rather, counties were created to provide basic services that are important to people whether they live in rural or urban areas. Every part of North Carolina is a part of one of the state's 100 counties.

When you think of county government, you might visualize the courthouse. The county's central offices are usually located in the courthouse. Official records of births, deaths, marriages, divorces, and property—sometimes stretching back hundreds of years—are maintained there. But county government does not stop at the courthouse steps. Counties operate facilities ranging from health care clinics to jails.

mandated service: a program which local governments must provide because of requirements from state or federal government

There are two kinds of services that counties provide. Just as cars come with standard equipment and can also have optional equipment added, all counties provide some standard services and can also offer optional services. The standard services must be provided under state law. Because the state requires them, they are called **mandated services.** Part of the reason that the General Assembly has divided the state into counties is to ensure that every resident of North Carolina will have easier access to mandated services through his or her county government. In this way, you might think of your county as a "branch office" of the state government.

But counties do more than carry out state requirements. Like cities and towns, counties are a special kind of corporation, with the power to own property, to

Chowan County's courthouse, built in 1767, is the state's oldest courthouse still in use.

enter into contracts, and to levy taxes. As local governments, counties have authority to regulate certain personal behavior (development of land or disposal of trash, for example), to encourage county improvement, and even to provide many of the same services cities and towns provide. In addition to the mandated services they must provide, most counties also adopt regulations, encourage community improvement, and provide other services. Depending on the needs of the area and the requests of local citizens, county officials may decide to provide various **optional services.** For example, water and sewers, or parks and recreation are becoming more popular services for counties to provide.

Most county services are available to all county residents, whether they live inside or outside a city or town. However, some services may be provided only to the **unincorporated** part of the county (the area outside city or town limits). For example, because most municipalities have their own police department, the county sheriff's department usually provides police patrol and criminal investigation only in unincorporated areas.

In this chapter, we will see how North Carolina's 100 county governments developed and how they are organized. We will also take a look at services provided only by counties. Chapter 4 will discuss other services that may be provided by either municipalities or counties.

History of North Carolina Counties

North Carolinians are especially proud of their counties and often identify themselves by the county where they live. Although county governments are similar in many ways, each county has a distinct personality that reflects the character and history of the people who live there.

Counties were a key part of colonial government in North Carolina. As British control and European settlement extended westward from the coast, the British authorities set up new counties to provide government for the colonists. The governor appointed justices of the peace in each county. The justices served as both the court and the administrators for the county. The justices of the peace appointed constables to enforce the law. They appointed a sheriff to collect taxes, and they appointed wardens to care for the poor. The justices also appointed a surveyor to mark land boundaries and a register of deeds to keep property records. Establishing land boundaries and maintaining records of property were very important to the farmers and planters who settled the colony. Having government officials nearby was especially important before the development of modern transportation, because it could take many hours to travel only a few miles.

optional service:
a program that a government decides to provide to meet the needs or requests of its residents

unincorporated:
the part of a county outside the cities and towns in that county

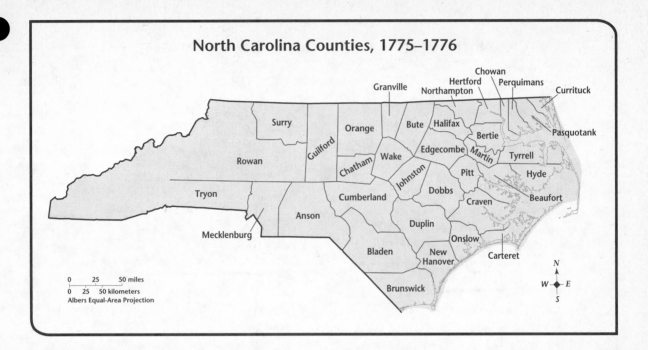

North Carolina Counties, 1775–1776

There were 35 counties in North Carolina when the state declared its independence from Great Britain in 1776. After independence, North Carolina state government continued to use counties to organize local citizens and provide basic government throughout the state. The General Assembly also continued to create new counties to bring government closer to the people. By 1800 there were 65 counties and by 1900 there were 97. In the twentieth century, only 3 additional counties were created to bring the total number of counties to 100.

Diverse North Carolina Counties

There is no "typical" North Carolina county. North Carolina's 100 counties are diverse. In area, they range from Chowan County (173 square miles) to Robeson County (949 square miles). The population differences are even greater. In 2000 Tyrrell County had the smallest population with just over 4,000 residents and Mecklenburg County had the largest population with more than 695,000 residents. Population density varies widely across counties too. Hyde County had only about 9 people per square mile, whereas Mecklenburg County had more than 1,300 people per square mile.

The land in the western part of the state is mountainous. Many of the **mountain counties** are heavily forested. The land is a flat **coastal plain** in the eastern part of the state. Some counties on the coastal plain are also heavily forested, but many are rich agricultural areas with many highly productive farms. Most of the mountain and coastal plain counties are **rural.** Agriculture and forestry are important economic activities in both parts of the state. Tourism is also especially important to the economy of the mountains and the coast. Fishing is important along the coast. There are few **urban** counties in

mountain counties:
the western region of North Carolina, extending eastward from the Tennessee border to the eastern boundaries of Alleghany, Wilkes, Caldwell, Burke, and Rutherford counties; includes 23 counties

coastal plain:
the eastern region of North Carolina, extending approximately 150 miles inland from the coast. The western border of the region is usually defined as the western boundaries of Northampton, Halifax, Nash, Johnston, Harnett, Hoke, and Scotland counties; includes 41 counties

rural:
of or relating to the country; area where fewer people live

urban:
area where people live close together; most incorporated as municipalities

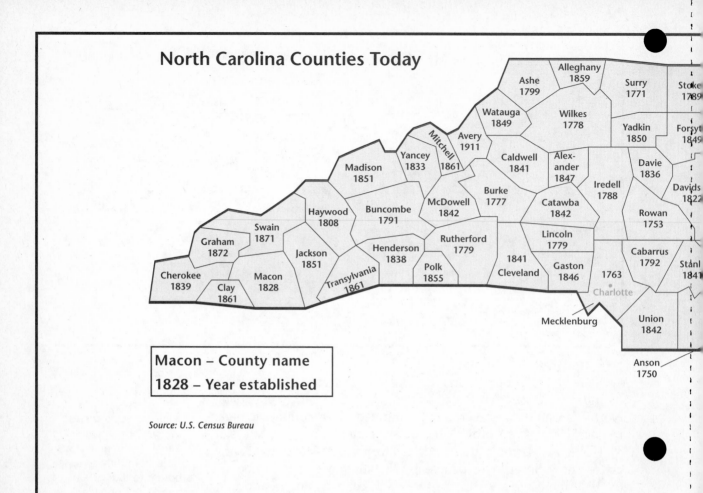

North Carolina Counties Today

Alleghany 1859
Ashe 1799
Surry 1771
Stokes 1789
Watauga 1849
Wilkes 1778
Yadkin 1850
Forsyth 1849
Mitchell
Avery 1911
Caldwell 1841
Alexander 1847
Davie 1836
Davidson 1822
Yancey 1833
Madison 1851
McDowell 1842
Burke 1777
Iredell 1788
Rowan 1753
Haywood 1808
Buncombe 1791
Catawba 1842
Swain 1871
Rutherford 1779
Lincoln 1779
Cabarrus 1792
Graham 1872
Jackson 1851
Henderson 1838
1841 Cleveland
Gaston 1846
1763
Stanly 1841
Cherokee 1839
Macon 1828
Polk 1855
Charlotte
Clay 1861
Transylvania 1861
Mecklenburg
Union 1842
Anson 1750

Macon – County name
1828 – Year established

Source: U.S. Census Bureau

piedmont:
the central region of North Carolina including Surry, Yadkin, Alexander, Catawba, and Cleveland counties on the west and Warren, Franklin, Wake, Chatham, Lee, Moore, and Richmond counties on the east; includes 36 counties

either area. Only Buncombe (Asheville) in the mountains, and Cumberland (Fayetteville) and New Hanover (Wilmington) on the coastal plain are predominantly urban and had more than 250 people per square mile in 2000.

The **piedmont,** in the central part of the state, is an area of rolling hills. North Carolina's biggest cities are in the piedmont. Ten piedmont counties are largely urban—Alamance, Cabarrus, Catawba, Durham, Forsyth, Gaston, Guilford, Mecklenburg, Orange, and Wake. However, most piedmont counties are largely rural. Farming is a more important part of the economy in the eastern piedmont counties than in the western piedmont counties. Manufacturing (especially of textiles, clothing, and furniture) is particularly important in the western piedmont counties, where even many rural counties have a considerable amount of industry.

Throughout the twentieth century, North Carolina's urban population has grown more rapidly than the rural population. As the bar graph on the next page shows, over half of the state's 8 million people lived in cities, towns, or villages by 2000.

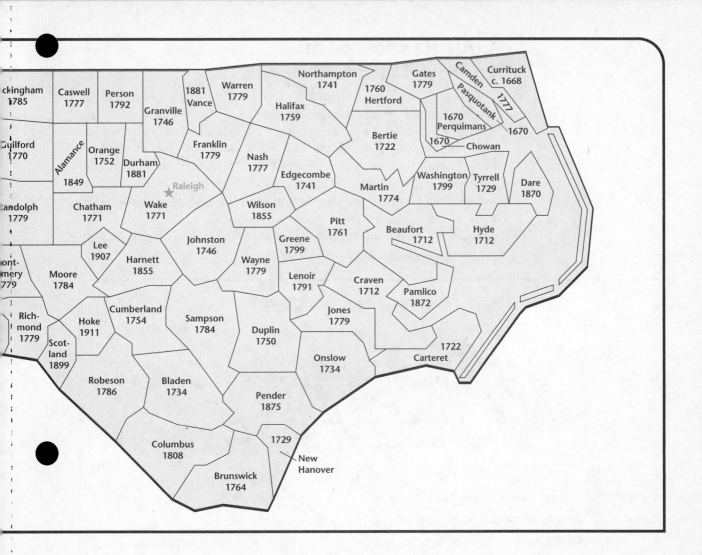

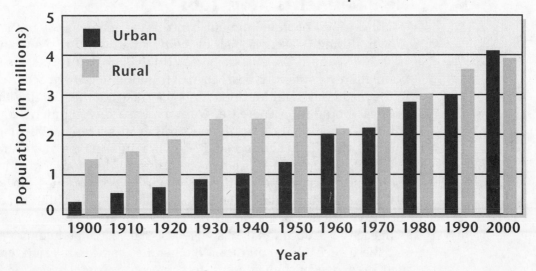

North Carolina's Rural and Urban Population, 1900–2000

Counties Respond to Population Changes

Population change greatly affects county governments. A change in the number of residents means a change in the demand for services, as well as a change in the amount of taxes needed to pay for those services. Since 1950 some North Carolina counties have become more densely populated, others have maintained their population, and still others have experienced a decrease in population. Overall, the population of the state doubled from 1950 to 2000, but most of that increase was concentrated in about half of the state's counties. The map below shows how each county's population changed during that time.

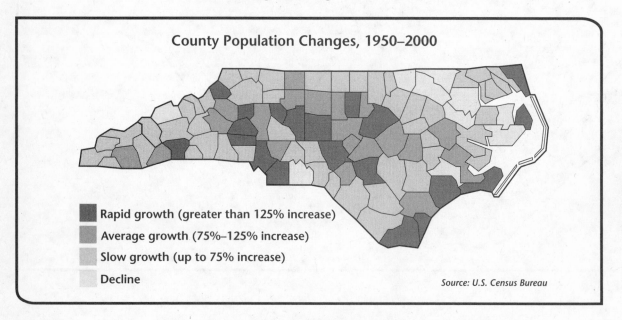

County Population Changes, 1950–2000

■ Rapid growth (greater than 125% increase)
■ Average growth (75%–125% increase)
■ Slow growth (up to 75% increase)
□ Decline

Source: U.S. Census Bureau

New Residents, New Jobs

Three kinds of development contributed most to population growth during the second half of the twentieth century. New and rapidly expanding businesses created jobs and led to increased population in some counties. Much of this kind of growth occurred in the piedmont, with Mecklenburg and Wake counties having the greatest population increase. Military base development contributed much to the population growth in some coastal plain counties, especially Cumberland (Fort Bragg) and Onslow (Camp LeJeune). Resort and retirement community developments also contributed to major population growth in several counties, particularly in the mountains (Henderson, Watauga) and at the beach (Brunswick, Currituck, Dare).

In each case, additional jobs were also created as people moved into these developing counties. Whether they came to take jobs created by expanding businesses, to serve on military bases, or to retire, new residents needed housing, food, clothing, banking, and other goods and services. This need led to the expansion of other businesses and to the creation of additional jobs.

As a result of the development of new jobs, people in counties with population growth generally have higher incomes than those who live in counties with little or no population growth.

In the
NEWS...

Chatham Department of Social Services Confronts Space Shortage

By Stephann Harris

The building that houses the Chatham County Social Services Department is busting out at its metal seams.

Employees are squeezed in[to] offices, sections of hallways have become veritable filing cabinets, and rooms meant for something else hold thousands of records.

"We don't have much room to add anymore," said Robert Hall, Chatham County Social Services director. "We have to put confidential files out in the halls."

It is uncertain how much relief the Chatham County Board of Commissioners will give them in the next few months as they decide what major projects will receive funding for the next fiscal year.

Social services officials are requesting a building expansion to accommodate the overcrowding, which stems from an increase in workload and employees. Cases for the Medicaid and Health Choice programs alone have increased by 300 over one year.

What ups the ante is the county's population growth. The Office of State Planning estimated that from 1990 to 1998, the population jumped by 19 percent. The growth is expected to continue, and more residents will undoubtedly create more need for social services. The department already serves an average of 170 families a week.

Social service workers have had to design creative ways to keep up the files. Because the 400-square-foot room for closed records is full, the department has had to convert a room and part of its conference room to store about 5,000 records. Apart from this, there are about 3,600 active records that either have to be placed in employees' offices or in filing cabinets in the halls.

The situation puts the department at risk of compromising privacy. Some of the files that are considered classified have to be kept in open areas.

Last month, the department invited the commissioners to tour the building to see the space shortage firsthand. Commissioner Uva Holland toured the social services building more than seven years ago and remembers concerns about space even then. She believes the board will come up with some kind of plan for relief.

"There's definitely a need for space. It's almost at an impossible stage now," Holland said. "We will have to find some ways to alleviate that."

There are 56 employees in the main building, originally designed for 46 people. Nine additional employees whose concentration is child-support services are in a rented house about a mile from the building at a cost of $1,500 a month.

Six of the offices in the main building are shared by two people. This temporary arrangement is not just inconvenient, it violates state regulations. The state's minimum requirement for workspace is 80 square feet for each staff person, or one office per employee. Even though the department is out of compliance, the state has shown flexibility because the expansion is included in the county's capital improvement plans.

—Excerpted with permission from *The News & Observer,* Raleigh, North Carolina, February 5, 2000.

Housing developments are springing up along the North Carolina countryside, creating some of the same problems that cities experience. Many counties have begun providing water, sewers, and other services to housing developments in unincorporated areas.

per capita:
equally to each person; by or for each person

Population growth creates the need for additional government services. Not only are there more people to be served, but the kinds of services needed may also change as the population increases. For example, housing developments outside city limits may require public water and sewer systems to protect the public health. New school buildings and other public facilities are also needed as the population increases. County governments must pay for these new facilities and hire new employees to serve their larger population.

Needs of Counties That Have Not Grown

In North Carolina, many counties that are primarily agricultural had little population growth or even experienced a decrease in population in the second half of the twentieth century. Machines replaced people for many farming operations during this period. In 1947, 42 percent of North Carolinians worked in agriculture. By 1987 only 3 percent of North Carolinians worked in agriculture. In some rural counties, manufacturing or tourist jobs replaced agricultural jobs. In other counties, however, there were few new jobs to replace those lost on the farms. These are the counties that lost population or had little population growth. These are also the counties where **per capita** income is lowest.

Counties with constant or declining population often have special problems. High unemployment and low wages mean that a larger proportion of the population needs financial assistance and health care from the county government. At the same time, poorer people pay less in taxes. A county with a low per capita income may have trouble raising funds to assist its needy residents.

Governing North Carolina Counties

Local voters in North Carolina could not select their own county officials until after the Civil War. Up until that time the state appointed county officials. The North Carolina Constitution of 1868 provided for the election of the sheriff, the coroner, the register of deeds, the clerk of court, the surveyor, and the treasurer. Under the 1868 constitution, voters in each county also began to elect a board of county commissioners. The board of county commissioners replaced appointed justices of the peace as officers of general government for the county. These county boards were responsible for the county's finances, including setting its tax rates.

Today, voters in each North Carolina county elect a board of county commissioners, a sheriff, a register of deeds, and a clerk of court. The clerk of court is no longer an office of county government, however. The General Assembly consolidated all county courts into a statewide court system, and the clerk, although elected by the county's voters, is an employee of the state courts. Judges and district attorneys are elected by judicial districts. Some judicial districts include only a single county, but in many cases

Working for Local Government

Bailiff Without a Gun Steps Down

By John Stevenson

The end of an era for the Durham Sheriff's Department and court system was observed Friday with the retirement of 72-year-old Joe Scott.

Scott's departure marked the final hurrah for a gentler, quieter time—a time when deputies armed with guns and pepper spray were not considered necessary to keep peace in court.

Scott was the last civilian courtroom bailiff in Durham and was believed by court officials to be the last in the entire state.

"It's kind of sad," Sheriff's Maj. Lucy Zastrow said of Scott's retirement.

"It ends a tradition," Zastrow added. "He's the last of a breed. But if we're going to lose the tradition, he's a hell of a good one to take it out. He's a very good man."

In addition to maintaining security, bailiffs must open court each day with a hearty "oyez, oyez, oyez"—the ancient call to order—and look after jurors, among other duties.

In Durham, no unarmed civilians have been hired as bailiffs since the early 1980s because judges, lawyers and clerks have worried about the rising potential for courtroom violence.

Such concerns have caused armed, uniformed deputies to be responsible for almost all courtroom security for two decades.

The last civilian holdouts were Scott, who was a bailiff for 18 years, and James Lofton Proctor, who retired in 2000 as the oldest bailiff in the state. Proctor was 85 when he left court work in Durham.

Those who know the bantamweight Scott say he never needed a weapon.

Scott is credited with almost magical people skills that enabled him to keep peace without a hint of force. With just a soft word or glance, he seemed to have a tranquilizing effect on everyone from loud-mouthed adult malcontents to screeching babies, court officials said.

Zastrow put it this way: "He is one of the most delightful people I've ever met. He looked at people not as defendants or plaintiffs in a

Bailiff Joe Scott was responsible for maintaining order in the courts for 18 years.

court case but just as people. He really wanted to help them, especially younger people. He wanted to get them on the right track. He considered his work to be as much a civil responsibility as a job. He will really be missed."

Still, Zastrow said, she understands the current doctrine that armed deputies rather than civilians should be used for courtroom security. Deputies also have powers of arrest that civilian bailiffs don't, Zastrow noted.

Sheriff's Lt. Jerry Harris, chief of courtroom security in Durham, said the elimination of civilian bailiffs is a "sign of the times."

"Things tend to be getting worse," said Harris. "You've got people who come up here and fight—gangs and stuff. You've got to have armed people now. When Mr. Scott started, people seemed to have more respect for the court system, more reverence."

"Armed bailiffs are trained to control conflict and are better able to do that," agreed Chief District Court Judge Kenneth C. Titus. "They can react appropriately when force may be necessary. Civilian bailiffs have been good at keeping tempers low. But some people have treated them with contempt. They won't be contemptuous to a deputy with a sidearm. Everybody feels safer when deputies

(Continued from page 31)

are around." Like others, Titus said Scott showed dignity and respect to all.

"Joe's been great," Titus added. "He has a calming influence on a rowdy crowd. Even without a weapon, he's been able to really help maintain order in the courtroom."

Titus said other communities in North Carolina did away with civilian bailiffs years ago, so Scott probably was indeed the last of his kind.

For his part, Scott said he hasn't carried a gun since he was a frontline infantryman during the Korean War 50 years ago, nor has he had any desire to carry one.

"I always felt perfectly comfortable without a gun," he said of his time as a bailiff. "I was never fearful because I didn't have a gun. Wearing a gun can make some guys mad. I think I was better off without one. To tell you the truth, I didn't want one. When I left Korea, I put the guns down for good."

Scott wasn't always a bailiff. He was a traveling salesman and businessman for 35 years, specializing first in beauty supplies and then auto parts, before he joined the Sheriff's Department.

He said he loved the "people-to-people" aspect of his work as a bailiff.

But he also said the trend toward increasing violence has not escaped his attention—a trend that included a recent shooting outside the courthouse. The shooting was linked to a hotly contested domestic lawsuit.

—Reprinted with permission from
The Herald-Sun, April 1, 2001.
© Durham Herald Company, Inc.

they include several counties. Regardless of the size of the judicial district, however, judges and district attorneys are state officials, not county officials. Voters also elect members of the local school board, which may cover an entire county, but sometimes includes only a part of a county. Thus, the county commissioners, the sheriff, and the register of deeds are the only county officials elected by voters in each of the 100 counties.

The Board of County Commissioners

The board of county commissioners has general responsibility for county government. It sets the local property tax rate and adopts the county budget. It passes ordinances, resolutions, and orders to establish county policies. Each board of county commissioners appoints a clerk to keep official records of the board's meetings and decisions, to publish notices, to conduct research, and to carry out other duties, such as providing information to citizens about their county government.

Unlike a city or town governing board, the board of county commissioners shares authority for setting county policy with other officials—state officials, the sheriff, the register of deeds, and independent county boards. The General Assembly and various state agencies are often directly involved in setting policy for county governments through mandates that require the county to provide certain services or follow specific procedures. As elected officials, the sheriff and the register of deeds have authority independent of the board of county commissioners and may set policies for their departments. Furthermore, state law provides for separate independent boards with responsibility for alcoholic beverage control, education, elections, health, mental health, and social services policy.

Independent Boards

The independent boards in North Carolina counties appoint directors for their agencies and make local policies regarding agency operations. Smaller counties may join together in a single health district or mental health area, with boards made up of representatives from each of the participating counties. Larger counties typically have their own health and mental health boards. In counties where alcoholic beverages may be sold, an Alcoholic Beverage Control (ABC) Board controls ABC stores in the county.

County social services boards hire a director for the county department of social services and advise the director on program needs and budget requests. Because many social service programs are funded by the United States government, federal and state regulations set much of the policy for social services delivered by counties.

The county elections board sets policies for operations of local voter registration and elections and selects an elections supervisor to manage these operations.

Most North Carolina counties have a single, countywide administrative unit for public schools, although some counties have more than one school system. Except for a few city school districts with appointed boards of education, the voters of each district elect the board of education for each school unit.

None of the independent boards has the authority to levy taxes. County funds to support these services must be raised by the board of county commissioners. All of the independent boards must also have their budgets approved by the board of county commissioners. The responsibility for financing operations and the power to control **expenditures** gives the board of county commissioners the ability to coordinate county policy for the services with independent boards. Because it raises and **allocates** county funds, the board of county commissioners has the potential to influence all government programs that depend on county money, including even the schools, which operate as separate administrative units.

expenditures:
money spent

allocate:
to set aside money for a specific purpose

The County Manager

In all North Carolina counties, the board of county commissioners hires a manager. The county manager directs the general operations of county government. He or she has the authority to hire and fire personnel in departments directly under the authority of the board of commissioners, but not those who are responsible to an independently elected official (sheriff, register of deeds) or work for the state personnel system or an independent board (education, elections, health, social services). The county manager prepares a budget for the county and manages the county's expenditures. He or she also reports to the board of commissioners on county government operations and on public problems facing the county.

Services Provided by County Governments

North Carolina counties provide many essential services for all North Carolina residents. The county register of deeds maintains legal records of all property transactions and of marriages, births, and deaths. The county board of elections registers voters and conducts elections. The county sheriff operates a jail to hold people awaiting trial and people convicted of minor crimes. Counties provide emergency medical services either through county departments or through support for volunteer emergency medical service squads. Counties also have responsibility for social services, public health services, and mental health services. Funding the public schools is also a major county responsibility.

Social Services

North Carolina counties have important responsibilities for assisting people with low incomes and other social problems. County departments of social services help children through programs like foster care, adoption, and family counseling. They investigate suspected abuse of children and disabled adults. They offer services to help the elderly and the disabled live at home, as well as programs to help people prepare for new jobs. County departments of social services often work closely with religious and other charitable organizations in providing these services.

In providing some services, the county must follow very specific regulations. For example, counties must operate **food stamps** and **Medicaid** programs according to strict federal regulations. Counties must follow these regulations in determining who is eligible to receive assistance from these programs and in organizing and operating their departments of social services to carry out the programs. In part, this is because counties pay only a portion of these programs. A majority of the funds for each of these programs comes from the U.S. government. To be eligible for funds from the U.S. government, states must have programs that meet federal requirements. Most of the 50 states use a department of state government to administer public assistance, but North Carolina is one of a few states that chose to assign the responsibility to counties. Still, the state (which also pays part of the cost) has to assure the U.S. government that federal requirements are being met. Strict regulation of county operations is one way to do this.

Another reason for strict regulation of public assistance programs is concern about welfare fraud. Many people believe that having very strict regulations will help ensure that only those who really need public assistance will receive these benefits. Others argue that too many regulations make it difficult for people to get the public assistance they need and also drive up the cost for those who do receive benefits.

food stamps:
a program to help people with financial need buy food; vouchers to be used like money for purchasing food; federal program, but administered by county departments of social services in North Carolina

Medicaid:
a program designed to pay for medical care for people in financial need; federal program, but administered by county departments of social services in North Carolina

In the NEWS...

Eastern Wake to Get Human Services Center

By Kristin Collins

Wake County officials have known for years that eastern Wake County needs more services such as counseling, substance-abuse programs and health care. Until now, the best they could do was to provide a few programs from a temporary building in the lot of Zebulon Middle School.

But this year the county will begin plans for a new $4.4 million regional center at the northern edge of Zebulon. The facility will bring human service programs long inaccessible to needy residents.

"I'm glad to hear it," Zebulon Commissioner Robert Holden said this week. "We need something in eastern Wake County. The way it is now, if you don't live on the other side of the Neuse River, you're kind of at a disadvantage."

Wake County leaders decided in 1994 to build four regional centers that would bring programs closer to residents. It was a major philosophical change for a county that traditionally had based its services in downtown Raleigh.

They studied factors such as teen pregnancy and infant mortality rates, school test scores and dropout rates, and decided the

most urgent need was in southern and eastern Wake [County], Sorrels said.

The first of the centers was built in Fuquay-Varina in 1996, and Zebulon was planned next. But the project didn't make it back onto the county's list of projects until this year, when $10.6 million was budgeted over the next seven years for regional centers.

Officials said planning for the Zebulon building would begin almost immediately, and construction could start next summer. They hope to open the doors in fall 2001. The remaining two centers are planned for Wake Forest and Apex in the next decade.

"It kind of ground to a halt for budgetary reasons," said Bob Sorrels, operations director for Wake Human Services. "This is the most hopeful that we've been in four years."

The eastern center will go on a campus that already is home to Zebulon Elementary School and a branch library. The county also plans to build a park nearby.

The center will provide human services such as mental-health and substance-abuse counseling, basic medical treatment, prenatal care and programs for children. Federal assistance programs including Medicaid, food stamps and Work First will be administered there.

In the same building, residents will be able to pay tax bills, access county records and file for environmental and building permits.

"Once those services come out there, people will begin to get the help they need," said Linda Coleman, eastern Wake's representative on the county Board of Commissioners. "I think it will have an impact on the whole economic structure."

Many of the services seem basic, but they have been out of reach for many who don't have the time or transportation to leave the community, local leaders and educators say.

School social workers in eastern Wake say many children, especially those who use Medicaid, never get the services they need

A young woman receives a medical exam at Wake County's temporary human services center in Zebulon.

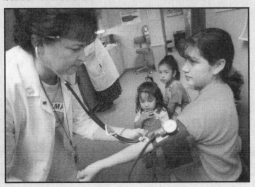

(Continued from page 35)

because parents aren't able to drive them to Raleigh.

"Everything we need for our kids to get mental-health help or even physical help, it's not here," said Kelly Lister, a social worker at Zebulon Middle School. "We don't have anything to offer except in Raleigh."

Officials hope the eastern center will ease those problems just as Fuquay-Varina's Southern Regional Center has. It serves thousands of clients each year.

Rosena West, director of Southern Regional, said the center has formed alliances with community service groups and drawn in clients who would not have gone to Raleigh for help. It has lured a branch of the state's Employment Security Commission, which provides job training and placement, and is piloting an education initiative with the Wake County Schools.

"We clearly see ourselves as part of the community, and being right there helps us to understand the problems the community is dealing with," West said. "This is a different way of trying to respond."

—Reprinted with permission from *The News & Observer*, Raleigh, North Carolina, August 11, 2000.

Temporary Assistance to Needy Families (TANF): federal government program of support for families in need; provides small payments to cover basic living expenses and assistance to help adults find and keep jobs

In order to provide greater flexibility in meeting people's needs for financial assistance, North Carolina counties also operate **Temporary Assistance to Needy Families (TANF)** programs. Under TANF, local departments of social services use federal, state, and local funds to provide support to families that do not earn enough money for basic living expenses. TANF can provide families money for a limited period of time while the parents find new jobs. TANF also provides job training so that people can qualify for higher paying jobs and helps pay for childcare, transportation, or other services the parents may need in order to keep a job.

Many counties have also established their own general assistance programs. These optional programs help people deal with emergencies and situations not covered by federal and state programs. The county social services board establishes the rules for general assistance in its county, and the board of county commissioners allocates county funds to pay for general assistance. Government programs do not cover all basic needs, however. Religious groups and other charitable organizations operate shelters for the homeless and for battered women; food banks and hot meals programs; clothing distribution centers; and other projects to meet the basic needs of those who cannot earn enough to provide for themselves. Some of these agencies also receive funding from county government to help them deliver specific social services.

Health

In North Carolina, each county is served by both a public health department and a mental health authority. Local public health departments work to improve people's health in three ways: they remove health hazards from the environment, they educate people and give shots to prevent illness, and they care for those who are ill and cannot afford to pay for care. Local mental health authorities provide services for people facing mental illness, developmental disability, or substance abuse.

Whether it is organized for a single county or for two or more counties, each local (public) health department must meet certain state mandates. It must inspect restaurants, hotels, and other public accommodations in the county to be sure that the facilities and the food are safe. It must also collect information and report to the state about births, deaths, and communicable diseases in the county.

Local health departments also typically provide many other services. They have programs to prevent animals, such as mosquitoes and rats, from spreading human diseases. Many health departments also enforce local sanitation ordinances for septic tanks or swimming pools and local animal-control ordinances. County nurses and health educators teach people about good nutrition and how to prevent illness. Most county health departments operate clinics to diagnose and treat illnesses and to provide health care for expectant mothers, infants, and children who cannot otherwise afford health care. County nurses also care for people in their homes and at school. They also give shots to prevent certain diseases.

Community-based treatment of mental illnesses, mental disabilities, and the abuse of alcohol and other drugs are operated by the area mental health authority (either a single-county board or a multi-county board). These services are another important part of each county's responsibilities for health education and care.

In Mecklenburg and Wake Counties, consolidated Human Services Departments bring together social services, public health, and mental health programs into a single department of county government.

Public Schools

In North Carolina, the public schools are both a state and a local responsibility. The state pays teachers' basic salaries and establishes qualifications for teachers. Teachers are considered state employees. The state does not hire teachers, however. Teachers are hired by local school boards, and local school boards are also responsible for deciding to keep or dismiss teachers.

The North Carolina State Board of Education establishes overall policies for the schools, including the minimum length of the school year, the content of the curriculum, and the textbooks that may be used. Local boards of education must meet the state's guidelines for school policy in all of their decisions about how the local schools will operate. Local school boards hire all local school personnel: teachers, staff, and administrators, including principals, superintendents, and their assistants. Local school boards decide what texts to use and what courses to offer. They set the calendar for the local schools and decide on school attendance policies.

Local school boards also adopt a budget for operating the schools. Although teachers' basic salaries are paid by the state, most other costs of the schools are a local responsibility. These include buildings, furniture, and equipment; books and other supplies; maintenance; and utilities. Many local school systems also pay teachers a salary bonus. The local school board decides how much it needs to spend to support the local schools. Then it presents this budget to the board of county commissioners. The school board has no authority to tax. The county commissioners decide how much county money to spend to support local schools. In most counties, schools receive the largest share of county money. Sometimes there is considerable discussion between the school board and the commissioners about how much money the schools should receive.

Each local school board hires a superintendent to coordinate planning for the schools, to select teachers and other school staff, to prepare and administer the budget, and to provide general administrative direction for the schools. Each school has a principal who has similar responsibilities for that school. In many parts of the state, schools are also beginning to involve teachers and parents more directly in helping plan for the school and in making decisions about how the school is run. Some schools also have advisory committees of people from local businesses and other members of the community.

The public schools have the responsibility of helping their students prepare for life. Some public school programs help prepare students directly for work. Other programs help students prepare for college. All public school programs should result in making students responsible citizens—people who take pride in their community and help make it a better place to live and work.

Public Facilities

Counties must also provide certain public facilities. Each county's board of county commissioners is required by the state to build and maintain a jail and to provide adequate office space for other mandated services. In addition, the board of county commissioners is responsible for providing suitable space and equipment for the state's district and superior courts.

Dealing With Changing Mandates

When the state requires counties to provide a service, the county must carry out that mandate. Mandates change, however. The General Assembly has changed counties' service responsibilities many times over the years. For example, one early responsibility of county governments in North Carolina was the construction and maintenance of rural roads and bridges. During the 1930s, however, the General Assembly transferred all responsibility for rural roads and bridges to the state highway department, now the North Carolina Department of Transportation.

Counties get new responsibilities too. In the late 1980s, the General Assembly passed laws requiring all counties to provide for the safe disposal of solid wastes produced in the county. This new mandate put all 100 counties in the business of managing solid waste. Many counties for the first time began programs to recycle, reuse, or compost solid wastes or to encourage people to create less waste material.

North Carolina county government is complex. The Board of County Commissioners has general responsibility for the county's finances and for many county services. However, state mandates, independently elected officials, and other independent boards also determine policy for many county-funded services. Counties are both local governments and divisions of state government. Counties are local governments in that they provide a government through which citizens can address local problems and opportunities. Counties are also a division of state government because they have to carry out many state programs that are mandated by North Carolina state law. Regardless of where you live in North Carolina, county government helps to shape your daily life.

Discussion Questions

1. Find your county on the map on pages 26–27. Now try to locate your county on the map on page 25. Had it been formed as a county by 1775?

   If not, what county was it part of?

2. What do you know about how your county was formed and how it got its name? You can find this information at the library or county historical society.

3. Locate your county on the map on page 28. What changes in population has your county experienced since 1950?

4. How many municipalities are in your county?

   What is your county's population?

   What proportion of county residents live inside incorporated areas?

   What proportion live in unincorporated areas?

5. How important is each of the following to your county's economy?

   agriculture

   manufacturing

   tourism

   military bases

   hospitals, colleges and universities, or other institutions

   banking and insurance

   warehouses and retail stores

   transportation

   fishing

   forestry

   What are the major employers in your county? What is the current unemployment rate? What kinds of jobs are most readily available in your county?

6. What county services have you or people you know used in the past month? How have these services affected you, even if you have not used them yourself?

7. Who are your county commissioners?

8. What major issue is your board of county commissioners currently discussing? Will this issue have an effect on you or your family? If so, what is the effect?

9. How does your county government cooperate with other local governments?

Public Services

- You turn the handle on the faucet and water flows into your glass.
- You put your trash out, and it is picked up and carried away.
- You play ball or swim in the pool at the park.
- You call the police or sheriff about a break-in at your house, and an officer comes to investigate.

Safe drinking water, regular trash collection, recreation opportunities, and police protection are among the many services provided by local governments. You and your family may use some of these services—water, for example—many times each day. Other services, such as trash collection or recreation, may be used only once or twice a week. Still other services—criminal investigations, for instance—may be used only rarely but are available whenever you need them.

The chart on page 41 lists the major services that North Carolina county and municipality governments have authority to provide under state law. No one government provides all of the services on this list. As we saw in the last chapter, counties must provide certain mandated services. Except for the mandated services, municipalities and counties choose which services they will provide, depending on the needs and interests of their citizens.

In this chapter you will go "behind the scenes" to see how a few public services are produced. You will look at water and sewer services, trash (solid waste) collection and disposal, recreation, and policing. These services are just examples of the many services local governments provide. Counties, cities, and towns also operate public libraries, provide fire protection, support hospitals, maintain animal shelters, and conduct many other public services.

Often local governments provide these services themselves. For example, they set up departments to operate water supply facilities, to collect trash, or to police the community. Sometimes, however, local governments hire a private business, a non-profit organization, or another government to produce a service. Government hiring of a business to produce a public service is called **privatization.** The government buys the service from the business rather than hiring government employees to produce the service.

privatization:
government buying a service from a business instead of producing the service itself

Major Services Provided by Counties and Municipalities in North Carolina

This chart shows a general listing of the services local governments are authorized to provide. Counties and municipalities may choose to contract for these services rather than operate them directly.

Services Usually Provided by Counties Only

1. Community colleges
2. Cooperative extension
3. Court facilities (construction and maintenance only)
4. Elections
5. Jails
6. Mental health services
7. Public health services
8. Public schools
9. Register of Deeds
10. Social services
11. Soil and water conservation
12. Tax assessment
13. Youth detention facilities

Services Provided by Both Counties and Municipalities

1. Airports
2. Ambulance service
3. Animal shelters
4. Art galleries and museums
5. Auditoriums/coliseums
6. Building inspection
7. Buses/public transit
8. Cable television regulation
9. Community and economic development
10. Community appearance
11. Emergency management
12. Environmental protection
13. Fire protection
14. Historic preservation
15. Human relations
16. Industrial development
17. Job training
18. Law enforcement
19. Libraries
20. Open space and parks
21. Planning, land use regulation, and code enforcement
22. Property acquisition, sales, and disposition
23. Public housing
24. Recreation programs
25. Rescue squads
26. Senior citizen programs
27. Sewer systems
28. Solid waste collection and disposal
29. Storm drainage
30. Tax collection
31. Veterans' services
32. Water supply and protection

Services Usually Provided by Municipalities Only

1. Cemeteries
2. Electric systems
3. Gas systems
4. Sidewalks
5. Street lighting
6. Streets
7. Traffic control
8. Urban development

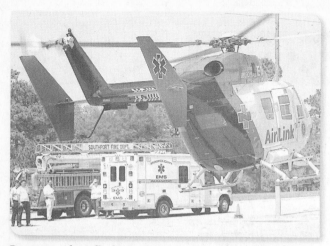

Rescues and medical emergencies often require the joint efforts of volunteers and paid emergency personnel.

Regardless of who produces public services, however, government pays for them. Governments raise most of the money to pay for services through taxes. For some services, the local government charges users of the service to help cover the cost of providing the service. For example, most governments charge their customers for the water they use.

Many public services are beneficial to its customers—the people who use them. For example, as a customer you can drink clean water, get rid of your trash, swim in the pool, or have a crime investigated. These are called "user-focused" services.

Many of these services also benefit the community at large. Having a safe, abundant water supply protects everyone in the community from diseases spread by contaminated water and also supports fire fighting. Safe, efficient waste collection and disposal helps keep the community healthy and attractive. Public recreation also supports a healthier, happier community. Criminal investigation helps protect the entire community from crime. Thus, public services benefit you both as an individual user and as a member of the community.

Water Supply

The water supply cycle involves four things or steps: source, treatment, distribution, and wastewater treatment. First, water is pumped from the source into a treatment plant where it is treated to make it safe to drink. Then the water is pumped into storage tanks, from which it is distributed through pipes to the people who will use it. Finally, wastewater is treated. Controlling water pollution is important to ensure a safe supply of drinking water. Sewage collection and treatment systems are essential to safe water supply systems.

Water Supply Sources

Wells are one important source of water in North Carolina. Wells tap into underground water. They allow water to be pumped out of the layers of sand, gravel, or porous rock, where it is trapped. In places where there are large pockets of underground water, wells can provide a steady source of water for public water systems. Rain and other water on the surface of the earth seeps down to replace the **ground water** that is pumped out. In rural areas where there is no public water system, each house may have its own well. Towns also use wells to supply public water systems where ground water is abundant.

ground water: water that collects underground

Rivers and reservoirs are other important water sources for public water systems. North Carolina has many rivers, and frequent rainfall ensures that they flow all year long. Some cities located near a river simply pump their water from the river. Where there is no convenient river with enough water, reservoirs must be built to catch and hold rainwater until it is needed. Most of North Carolina's larger cities, and many smaller ones, depend on water from reservoirs. Water from rivers, reservoirs, lakes, and so on, is called **surface water.** All of the land that drains into a reservoir is called the **watershed** for that reservoir. Watershed protection can reduce contamination of rivers and reservoirs, but surface water is still likely to be more contaminated than ground water.

Reservoirs are much more expensive water sources than either wells or rivers. Building a reservoir requires buying the land, which will be flooded by the new lake, and constructing a dam to contain the water. Engineers must first design a dam and map out the area the new lake will cover. Then the agency building the reservoir can begin to buy the land. Many reservoirs are built specifically to supply water. Some dams that provide water are built for other purposes, however. The federal government, working through the Army Corps of Engineers, builds reservoirs for flood control. Some private companies build reservoirs for electric power generation. If a city has to build its own reservoir, the cost of the reservoir is paid by the customers who use the water. Thus, cities that must build reservoirs to ensure an adequate supply of water usually have higher water rates than cities that are able to get all the water they need from wells or rivers.

The most expensive method of supplying water is using seawater. Along the coast, a few communities take the salt out of sea water through a process called **desalinization.**

Water Treatment

The kind of treatment water needs depends upon the **impurities** in it. Water from wells sometimes has almost no impurities. It has been filtered naturally as it collects underground. On the other hand, underground water can become contaminated if harmful substances are buried nearby. To help prevent contamination of ground water, the federal government has passed several environmental protection laws. One outlaws the discharge of dangerous chemicals into a stream or into the soil. Another requires landfills to be lined so that water cannot seep out of them and carry materials into the ground water. Still another requires underground storage tanks (such as those for gasoline) to be rustproof so they will not leak.

Surface water picks up such things as oil and grit from streets and parking lots; the fertilizer and pesticides from fields, trash or waste that is left exposed; and even soil particles. Therefore, surface water generally requires more treatment than well water. The first step in treating surface water is to filter it.

surface water:
all waters on the surface of the Earth found in rivers, streams, lakes, ponds, and so on

watershed:
an area that drains water into a stream or lake

desalinization:
the process by which the salt is taken out of sea water

impurities:
materials that pollute

Water plant tours help visitors understand the process of making water safe for people to drink.

At the water treatment plant, filtering and sedimentation remove solid particles from the water. (Sedimentation involves adding chemicals to the water that cause the suspended solids to clump together and sink.) The water must next be treated chemically to kill harmful bacteria. Chlorine compounds are typically added to the water for this purpose. In many places, fluorine compounds are also added to the water to reduce tooth decay. Water plant operators must constantly monitor the water through each stage of treatment to be sure they are adding just the right amount of each of the chemicals they use.

Water Distribution

Treated water is pumped into elevated storage tanks so that it can flow through underground pipes to all the places it will be used. Each house, school, office building, store, or factory using water from the public water system is connected to the water distribution lines. Another expense in providing a public water supply is the construction of the water lines.

A meter at the point of connection measures how much water flows out of the line and into each customer's property. These meters are read periodically, and the customer is billed for the water that has passed through the meter.

Besides distributing water to users, the water lines provide another benefit. Fire hydrants connected to the lines give firefighters ready access to water used in fighting fires. Public water systems need to deliver enough water for fire fighting, as well as enough for residential, commercial, and industrial uses.

Sewage Collection and Treatment

The liquid wastes from houses, schools, stores, offices, and factories are potentially dangerous. If they are not treated, these wastes can contaminate water with the chemicals or bacteria they carry. To avoid contaminating drinking water, hazardous chemicals, such as oil and many industrial and cleaning products, should not be poured on the ground or down the drain.

septic tank:
a container in which wastes are broken down by bacteria

In some areas, drains go into **septic tanks** in which harmful bacteria are killed by natural processes. In these areas each house usually has its own septic tank. However, septic tanks cannot be used in densely populated areas or in areas where the soil will not readily absorb the water that has been treated in the tank. In these areas, wastewater should be collected in sewers, which deliver it to a sewage treatment plant.

Working for Local Government

But Somebody's Got to Do It

By Eleanore Hajian

James Evans and Chris Cockman know when something stinks. They're sleuths of sorts, on a seek-and-destroy mission for roots, grease and other obstructions in the sewer lines of Southern Pines.

"When you go to the ones with the grease clogs, now those get really bad," Evans said. "Everything gets all backed up and just sits and then that's just the worst."

The men describe their other arch nemesis like something out of a science fiction movie.

"Trees will find water in winter wherever it is," said Evans.

"Yeah . . . they send out these feeder roots no bigger than a hair on your head and they go looking for water," said Cockman.

"They'll go and go until they find water. They'll work their way into a pipe, that tiny root will do that," said Evans. "When they find it— they stay there and start to grow, and it will get as big as your thigh."

The grease isn't hard to find. Certain manholes get a reputation for that sort of thing.

"Grease will get as hard as a rock in the winter," said Cockman pointing at some black chunky material in a manhole he had just flushed out with a specially designed high-powered hose.

Following the washing, the water flowed swiftly through the manhole. But earlier, it had been stagnant.

Cockman and Evans used what's known as "The Truck" to get the job done. Cockman, an equipment operator II, is one of a few public works employees with the Class A license needed to drive the 60,000 pound, 31-foot-long sewer cleaning and vacuum truck. The truck comes equipped with a special high-pressure hose that shoots its way through sewer lines, a smaller version of the same hose for the little lines that lead to people's homes, a giant vacuum tube for removing solids or sucking up large amounts of water when leaks prevent access to pipes, and few other gadgets.

To get out the grease and debris previously loosened by another team that works a router type device, Cockman pulled the truck up to the manhole. Then Evans took a sledgehammer to the manhole cover to loosen it.

"They got pavement on it and it's stuck on there real good," he said as he pounded down again and again. Cockman assisted by prying with a large hook.

Once they got the cover off, they swung the big hose out. Then using a feeder tube, they lowered the hose into the sewer line and started the high-pressure water that sometimes contains solvent to

James Evans, Chris Cockman, and "The Truck"

(Continued from page 45)

break down the grease. Slowly, they lowered the hose as it went further and further up the sewer line. Then it was time to pull the hose out. Equipped with latex gloves, goggles, hard hat and dressed in hard-to-penetrate work clothes, Cockman slowly pulled out the hose until he could see the end come out of the sewer line.

Despite the icky occurrences, Evans and Cockman will tell you that their job is not bad. Both do a variety of jobs in the merged sewer and water maintenance department, but working the truck is one of their specialties.

"You get out here and you basically know what you've got to do," said Cockman. "There's not a lot of people looking over your shoulders, and you're your own boss. If you don't do your job right, people know it pretty quick."

—Excerpted with permission from *Southern City,* January 2001.

At the sewage treatment plant, chemical and biological processes eliminate harmful chemicals and bacteria from the wastewater and separate solids from the liquid wastes. The solid material separated from sewage is called **sludge.** Properly treated sludge is safe to use for fertilizer and is often recycled in that way. Properly treated water is safe to release into rivers or lakes. It is safe to drink and becomes a part of the water supply for residents farther downstream.

sludge:
the solid material separated from sewage

Public Water Systems

Most cities and towns operate their own water supply and wastewater systems. An increasing number of counties have also begun to operate water distribution and sewage treatment facilities in areas where wells and septic tanks cannot provide safe water and safe wastewater disposal. Some cities and counties cooperate with one another in producing water or sewage services. In a few parts of the state, special water and sewer agencies have been created by local governments to operate water and sewer facilities for the entire area. Examples include the Charlotte-Mecklenburg Utility District and the Orange Water and Sewer Authority. Other counties, such as Catawba, loan money to local municipalities so that they can extend water service to unincorporated areas.

Solid Waste Management

Everything you no longer want or need has to go somewhere. The solid wastes you generate—old newspapers, food scraps, used packaging, grass clippings—have to be disposed of safely. Chemicals from casually discarded trash can contaminate water. Garbage and

A crew working under contract to the city paints this water tower in Southport.

In the NEWS...

Cumberland Board OKs Water Planning

By Andrew Barksdale

Cumberland County agreed to hire a consultant who will plan a countywide public water system.

The commissions voted to give $58,650 to the Raleigh engineering firm of Camp Dresser & McKee. Last week, the Public Works Commission approved spending an additional $228,050 on the firm's study.

The county and the PWC are sharing the costs, because both want to help bring service to rural areas.

Commissioner Tal Baggett said the county lags behind its neighbors who have countywide water systems, so the study is badly needed. He said that members of the board in the 1970s failed to take advantage of federal money available for such a project.

Lee Warren, the board's vice chairman, agreed. "The leaders of that time did not see that as a strong priority, and that is the reason we have been behind ever since," he said. It is going to take us some aggressive measures to take us where we need to be."

County Engineer Bob Stanger said the study will focus on identifying where to build future water lines and developing the organization and funding sources that a countywide water system would need.

The study will also determine how many water and sewer districts the county needs and where to put them. That answer is the key in finding money to extend public service, officials said.

Districts can apply for federal Rural Development grants and low-interest loans toward the cost of new water and sewer lines. People living in those districts can hold bond referendums to raise additional money.

The county commissioners agreed that the Kelly Hills area north of Fayetteville badly needs public sewers. The area, which includes Slocomb Road, has wet clay that causes smelly drainage from septic tanks that seeps to the surface when it rains. They asked County Manager James Martin to see what financial help may be available to help Kelly Hills as soon as possible.

Neighbors first asked the county three years ago for financial help for installing a public sewer. A county consultant reported in September that the project would cost $2.9 million, which the county does not have.

Officials say the county has several unincorporated communities without public water and sewer. The commissioners agreed with Baggett that the county should avoid a proliferation of small districts because of the time and legal work needed to form them. Baggett said grouping rural neighborhoods into larger districts is better planning.

The county's only sanitary district in Eastover has 11,420 acres and 1,045 households that have volunteered to hook into the district's water system. The proposed Kelly Hills sanitary district has 340 acres and 140 property owners.

Commissioner Breeden Blackwell suggested the board start putting money aside for future water and sewer projects. In anticipating the study's results, he asked Martin to prioritize the communities that most need public water or sewer. The study's final results will take a year.

—Excerpted with permission from *The Fayetteville Observer*, October 17, 2000.

trash also create a health hazard by providing a home for rats and other disease-bearing pests. Burning trash does not solve the problem of safe disposal because burning can pollute the air.

Local government helps solve the problem of safe disposal of solid waste. But safe (and low cost) solid waste disposal also requires your cooperation and that of everyone in the community.

The least expensive way to deal with waste is simply not to create it in the first place. Cutting out the use of packaging and disposable items, for example, can reduce waste considerably.

In addition to encouraging waste reduction, local governments help solve the solid waste problem in three other ways. They support recycling, help collect trash and garbage, and provide sanitary landfills or incinerators so that wastes that cannot be recycled are safely buried or burned. Participation by the public is most important for recycling and waste collection.

Recycling

Recycling wastes means using them as a resource to make new products. Thus, waste paper can be recycled to make new paper and old glass bottles can be recycled to make new bottles. In order to recycle materials, they must be separated—the paper from the glass, for example. Some recycling can be done at home. For instance, grass clippings and leaves can be turned into **compost** or **mulch**. One problem is that most people are not used to sorting their trash or reusing it at home, but that is changing.

Local governments encourage recycling by urging people to separate materials that can be recycled and by telling people how they can reuse materials. They also support recycling by collecting recyclable materials. Some local governments pick up materials for recycling by sending collection crews out to houses. An alternative is for local governments to operate recycling centers where people can deliver their recyclable materials.

Most of the manufacturing of new products from discarded materials is done by private industry. Paper companies use wastepaper to make new paper. Glass companies use discarded bottles to make new bottles. Local governments that collect these recyclables sell them to the manufacturing companies. The money the governments receive from these sales helps pay for the cost of collecting the materials. Some cities and counties are also actually making recycled products themselves. Several cities and counties have begun to use yard wastes (grass clippings, leaves, chipped wood) to make compost or mulch. Local governments also support recycling by buying products made of recycled materials. By using recycled paper, for example, the governments create a greater demand for the old newspapers to sell to the companies that make recycled paper.

Governments support recycling to protect natural resources. Government officials also have a more direct interest in recycling: saving money. Burying trash in a sanitary landfill is very expensive. Burning solid wastes safely is even more expensive. Recycling is an excellent way to save money because it reduces the amount of material going into landfills.

compost:
decayed material that is used as a fertilizer

mulch:
material spread around plants that prevents the growth of weeds and protects the soil from drying out

Local governments encourage recycling.

In the NEWS...

County Landfill Will Open Drywall Recycling Center

By Demorris Lee

Wake County has closed one of its yard waste disposal facilities in an effort to capture another market of recyclable goods—building goods.

The county is hoping to take advantage of the area's housing boom by providing a drywall recycling facility at North Wake Landfill.

Marshall Parrish, an education specialist with Wake's Solid Waste Management Division, said the market is prime for construction and demolition debris.

"Recycling markets fluctuate, and now the market is strong for drywall," Parrish said.

To house the recycling facility, the county stopped taking yard waste at North Wake. That area of the landfill will be retrofitted to handle commercial-construction and demolition debris.

Though county officials are looking to capture a new market, some residents are unhappy that they will have to drive farther and pay to dispose of their branches, grass and weeds. Before August 26, yard waste could be disposed of for free at North Wake.

"We are just out of luck," said George Mitchell, who lives off Ray Road. "Not only

will we have to drive 20 to 30 miles, but we also have to pay."

Mitchell said he is especially concerned because he has a huge yard with pine trees that can require several trips to the landfill. Plus, his home is not within the City of Raleigh, where there is free curbside pickup of yard waste.

Northern Wake residents can now take their yard waste to the city's facility at 900 New Hope Road for $420 per ton or to the Rowland Landfill at 3000 Gresham Lake Road. The price there depends on the length of a truck's bed.

Wayne Woodlief, the county's solid waste director, said that when the county started accepting yard waste in 1993, there were not many facilities in the area offering the service.

"There are now sufficient facilities around," he said. "That afforded us the opportunity . . . to implement this program."

Woodlief said 22 percent of the waste at the landfill is from the construction industry. The majority of that is drywall and wood waste, he said.

Under the new operation, contractors, builders and residents will be able to dispose of construction and demolition debris for $20 a ton if they separate out drywall and sheetrock, which are recyclable.

For unseparated debris, builders must pay $37 per ton at the North Wake Landfill and $25 per ton at the Feltonsville Landfill south of Apex.

All drywall must be clean, dry and unpainted, and loads must be free of trash, dirt, wood and other debris.

Woodlief said that Waste Industries will manage the transfer station and will take the material to Goldston, where it will be recycled. The recycled materials can be reused in the manufacture of products for landscaping and agriculture, such as oil absorbents and soil amendments for golf courses.

—Excerpted with permission from
The News & Observer, September 1, 2000.

Kenneth Patterson, president of Packer Industries, Inc., talks with John Blaisdell of the NC Department of Environment and Natural Resources about the uses of the Packer 750 horizontal grinder.

Solid Waste Collection

Most cities and towns provide for house-to-house collection of solid waste. Once or twice a week, the "garbage truck" comes down each street and the crew empties the trash from the cans outside each house. (Usually, these are city crews and trucks. In some municipalities, however, the city hires private companies to collect solid wastes.) The truck, called a "packer," is specially designed to crush the waste and press it together tightly so that it takes up as little space as possible.

Recycling collections are usually made on a different day and with another kind of truck. The recycling truck has bins for different sorts of material. As the recycling crew empties the containers of recyclables left outside each house, they separate the different kinds of materials. Most larger municipalities and some counties have door-to-door recycling collections.

Most counties and many small towns do not provide house-to-house solid waste collection. Instead, residents of unincorporated areas either hire a private company to collect their trash or they take it to a waste collection site themselves. Bins for recyclable materials are also often placed at waste collection sites. Most counties operate several waste collection sites. Sometimes the waste collection site consists of a large (usually green) box into which people put their trash. The box is emptied regularly into a very large packer truck. But if the box is not emptied often enough, or if people are not careful how they handle their trash, waste can spill out of the box. "Green box" sites can become very smelly trash-covered places and create health hazards.

An alternative is the supervised waste collection site. Supervised sites have a packer right on the site. The packer operator sees that people put their trash into the packer, which immediately crushes the trash. Both the supervision and the immediate packing of the waste help prevent the mess and hazard of "green box" sites.

Some dangerous materials require special handling. State and federal regulations prohibit radioactive wastes and hazardous chemicals from being mixed with other solid wastes. These materials (including motor oil; paints; and other household chemicals, tires, and batteries) must be kept separate and cannot be collected through the regular collection system. You, your family, and other people in the community are responsible for sorting out these materials and making sure that they are collected appropriately.

Solid Waste Disposal

Once solid waste has been collected, local governments must dispose of it. Wastes can be recycled, burned, or buried. Each of these disposal methods requires special equipment and techniques to assure public safety. In North Carolina, each county is responsible for making sure solid wastes produced in the county are disposed of safely. Most counties operate their own landfills. Some counties hire private businesses or contract with cities to dispose of their solid wastes.

Some recycling can occur from wastes that have been mixed together. In a materials recovery operation, people sort through the solid wastes that have been collected, and pick out things such as glass and cardboard. Then the remaining wastes can be passed through magnets to remove iron and through another process to remove aluminum. Materials recovery from mixed waste is done rarely because it is very expensive. Separation at the source is much less expensive and much more frequently done, but it requires active public support to be effective.

The safe burning of wastes is also quite expensive. This process is called **incineration** and requires very special equipment. First, materials that will not burn (glass, metal, and rock, for example) must be sorted out. Then the burnable materials must be shredded. Special furnaces are required to burn the wastes at very high temperatures so that as many harmful chemicals as possible are destroyed by the fire. There is some smoke, however, even from a very hot, clean-burning fire. This smoke must be filtered and treated carefully to prevent air pollution.

incineration:
the safe burning of wastes

The most common way to dispose of solid waste is to bury it. Safe burial of wastes requires the construction and operation of a sanitary landfill. State and federal regulations require that solid wastes be buried only in a properly constructed landfill. Special care must be taken to assure that the landfill does not pollute surface water or ground water. The landfill pit must be lined with plastic so that rainwater will not carry chemicals from the waste into the ground water. Any liquids or gases that do escape from a landfill must be captured and treated before being released. Each day's waste must be covered with soil so that animals that might spread diseases are not attracted to the site. No fires are allowed. When the landfill is finally full, it must be covered more deeply with soil, planted with grass or trees, and monitored to make sure that any leaking liquids or gases are properly treated. Landfill operators direct the unloading of waste and see that it is properly covered. They must be specially trained to ensure safe handling of the wastes.

The costs of the land, of constructing the landfill, and of operating it according to state and federal regulations are considerable. To help pay these costs, many counties charge users "tipping fees" for all the waste they unload in the landfill. Some cities and counties charge individual households or businesses for the costs of collecting and disposing of their solid waste. The more waste they produce, the more they pay. Other local governments finance solid waste collection and disposal with taxes. The public can help keep these costs as low as possible by cutting down on what they throw away, by sorting out recyclable materials from the rest of the trash, and by buying products made from recycled materials.

Recreation centers offer instructional programs for people of all ages.

Parks and Recreation

Many local governments provide recreational opportunities for their residents. They build and maintain parks, which may have picnic tables, swing sets, ball fields, basketball and tennis courts, swimming pools, or other facilities. They operate recreation programs, which may include organized sports leagues, supervised swimming, instruction in crafts or games, and physical fitness programs. Parks provide safe, attractive places for people to enjoy themselves and to relax. Recreation programs extend opportunities for healthful exercise and relaxation.

Parks and recreation programs are staffed by people with many different specialties. A supervised swimming program, for example, requires a staff of qualified lifeguards. Not only must they know lifesaving techniques, but they must also know how to operate the pool's filtering system and how and when to add chemicals to keep the water safe for swimming. They also need to know how to communicate well with pool users to assure safe use of the pool.

Similarly, the recreation assistants who referee games, teach sports, or lead crafts sessions need to know not only the rules and techniques specific to that activity, but also how to communicate effectively and to treat everyone fairly. Park maintenance workers use a range of skills to keep parks safe and clean. Park and recreation directors need to know about all of these operations and to plan and coordinate them. Many directors have studied recreation administration in college.

Well-maintained parks provide safe places for children to play.

Buying the land for a park, landscaping it, and building park facilities is a major investment for local government. Each park needs to be designed and built for heavy public use. After all, a park is a success only if people use it. But heavy use creates much wear and tear. Thus, parks also require constant maintenance. Equipment wears out and must be repaired or replaced. Keeping a park clean and in good repair costs money. Vandalism—the purposeful destruction of property—creates an even greater need for maintenance. Often a city or county does not have enough money to repair or replace park equipment that is broken before it would normally wear out.

People contribute to the success of a park by using it and by using it in ways that do not destroy the facilities or others' use and enjoyment of the park. Public cooperation is an essential part of every park and recreation program.

Police Protection

Local law enforcement officers are available to help every North Carolina resident. Except for some of the smallest towns, each municipality in the state has its own police department. Gaston County also has a police department, and Mecklenburg County and Charlotte have a merged police department. In the other 98 counties, sheriff's deputies provide police protection in unincorporated areas of the county and in towns without their own police department. Police officers and sheriff's deputies have similar duties and authority. In this section, we will often refer to them collectively as "police."

Police officers are required to go through specialized training. They study both criminal law (which defines illegal behavior) and constitutional law (which defines your rights). They learn how and when to use weapons and other self-defense measures. They learn how to gather information and evidence.

Police officers also study ways to communicate clearly and to understand, respect, and deal with the differences among people. In fact, communicating with people and responding to their concerns for safety are essential parts of police work. Most police officers realize that they need the respect and trust of the public to do their jobs well. The people and the police must work together to have safe communities. Police help protect you and your community in three ways. They investigate crimes, provide other emergency assistance, and conduct patrol and other crime prevention operations.

Criminal Investigation

Although crimes are defined by the state legislature, most of the criminal investigation and crime prevention work in North Carolina is done by local police departments and sheriff's departments. Most criminal investigations begin when the victim or a witness calls the police. In many cities and counties, a special emergency telephone number, 911, reaches police and sheriff's departments. (Fire departments and emergency rescue squads can generally be reached through the 911 number as well.) Trained telephone operators ask the caller to describe the problem and the location of the victim.

If the crime is in progress, if the victim is injured, if the crime is very serious, or if a suspect is still on the scene, the **dispatcher** will radio police to respond immediately. The caller will usually be asked to stay on the line to inform responding officers about changes in the situation and help direct them to the location.

Responding officers will stop any additional injury from happening and will make sure that emergency medical services are provided. The police will also arrest any suspects on the scene, interview the victim and witnesses about what happened, and inspect the scene. The officer in charge will then prepare an **incident report,** describing the crime and any suspects.

If a crime has already occurred, the caller might be asked to wait for police to arrive, to make an appointment to meet with police at a more convenient time, or to give a report about the crime over the phone. Often only a single officer is dispatched to interview the victim or witness to a crime that has already occurred.

After the responding officer interviews victims and witnesses and inspects the scene, he or she will write an incident report describing the crime and any suspects. Responding officers turn in their incident reports before they leave work each day. Their supervisors review these reports and decide which crimes should be investigated further. The most serious crimes are usually assigned to detectives who specialize in criminal investigation.

Criminal investigations seek to identify the person(s) suspected of the crime, to gather evidence that can be used in court to convict the suspect, to arrest the suspect, and to recover any stolen property. Public cooperation is essential to effective criminal investigations. In the first place, police rely on victims and witnesses to report crimes. Unless people are willing to tell police about incidents that appear to involve a crime, most crimes will never come to police attention. Moreover, most suspects are identified from witness accounts. Much of the work of criminal investigation is interviewing victims and witnesses to obtain as complete an account of the incident as possible. People must be willing and able to tell police what they saw if police investigations are to be successful.

Crime Prevention

A large number of police activities are intended to help prevent crime. Police patrols (usually by car; sometimes on foot, bike, or horse) help discourage crime by making police visible throughout the community. Police sometimes concentrate their patrols in areas

dispatcher:
a person who gives emergency workers information so that those workers can respond to emergencies

incident report:
a report that a police officer writes describing a crime or other problem situation

Working for Local Government

To Protect and To Serve: Officer Builds Bridge Between the Community and the Police

By Mark Schultz

A college textbook changed Charles Pardo's career path, and the now 33-year-old Chapel Hill police officer says he's never looked back.

Pardo was a student at East Carolina University studying business when he picked up one of his resident adviser's books.

"I started looking through this, and I said, 'Wow, this is really cool. What are you studying?'" Pardo recalled. "He said criminal justice."

A police officer for the past four years, Pardo joined the department's community services unit six months ago. He is one of three people in the unit, which focuses on crime prevention.

"As a patrol officer you don't always have time to do all the things you want to do; you're running from call to call," Pardo explained, sitting in his office at University Mall in Chapel Hill. "This [unit] gives us the ability to work more one on one."

Pardo is one of three Hispanic officers in the Police Department and one of about eight who are bilingual, he said. His parents, who are of Spanish descent, moved from New York City to Puerto Rico when he was 6 months old, and he lived there 21 years before coming to the United States for college.

He asked to work in community services because he could speak Spanish and wanted to work with the Latino community.

"A lot of Latinos are afraid of law enforcement. They sometimes feel law enforcement officers are racist," Pardo said.

"I'm not going to say that there are not people out there who are racist, but the main reason people get into law enforcement is to help people," he said. "Believe me, there are a lot more people out here who want to help."

Pardo frequently has to educate Latinos that the Police Department is not part of "La Migra," the Immigration and Naturalization Service. Police will forward reports to federal authorities in the case of serious felonies, "but we also do that with Anglos," Pardo said.

The Chapel Hill Police Department is just beginning to build a relationship with the Latino community, said Pardo's supervisor, Maj. Tony Oakley.

"Charlie brings knowledge of some of the problems, both cultural and language-wise, that the Hispanic population is feeling. He can relate to them. He knows where they are coming from," Oakley said.

—Excerpted with permission from *The Herald-Sun*, May 17, 2002.

Officer Charles Pardo

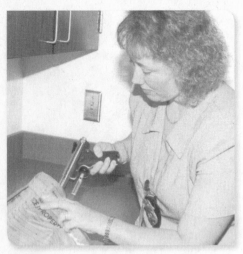

A police investigator bags a revolver as evidence.

where there have been frequent reports of crime. In addition to patrols, police attempt to prevent crime by informing people about ways to protect their property and themselves. Police also help people learn non-violent ways to solve arguments and find ways to avoid getting involved in criminal activities. After all, police cannot be everywhere at once. Crime prevention depends on the entire community.

Who Benefits From Public Services?

As you have seen, user-focused public services have both individual and community-wide benefits. If only the customer benefits, private business can provide the service. People will buy a service because they want it. No public money or authority is needed. Local governments provide services when public officials decide there are important community-wide benefits. These include the benefits of seeing that everyone has access to essential services, as well as improvements for the community as a whole.

Discussion Questions

1. Where does your drinking water at home come from? What is the source of the water? How is it treated? Who treats it? How is the water distributed? Who distributes it? How does your family dispose of wastewater from your house?

2. How does your family get rid of garbage, trash, and other solid waste? Do you recycle any of these materials? How does your local government help you dispose of solid waste?

3. When was the last time you used a city or county park or recreation program? What do you like best about your local parks? What would you change about your city or county parks and recreation program?

4. What local government provides police protection to the area where you live? Have you ever called on the police for help? What did they do in response to your request?

5. Which of the services listed in the chart on page 41 does your county provide or pay for?

Does the county provide or carry out each of these services itself or hire others to provide the service?

6. Which of the services listed in the chart on page 41 does your municipality provide or pay for? Does the municipality provide or carry out each of these services itself or hire others to provide the service?

7. Which services listed in the chart on page 41 are provided jointly by county and municipal governments where you live? Who provides these services?

8. Does any other government, private business, or community organization provide any of the services listed in the chart on page 41? What are they? How is the service provided by these organizations different than it would be if local government provided it?

9. What services would you like local government to provide differently than it does now?

5 Improving the Community

Making the community a better place to live is a major goal of local governments. In one way, of course, all public services help improve the community. As you learned in Chapter 4, user-focused services (like waste disposal and criminal investigation) help not only the people who use the service directly, but also their neighbors and even people who only work, shop, or travel through the community. Most public services help both people who use them directly and the community at large.

This chapter focuses on services that do not have direct users. These services are specifically intended to help make the entire community better. Planting flowers in public areas, encouraging **economic development,** and improving human relations are examples of these "community-focused" services. They are intended to change the physical, economic, or social setting in which people live and work. These services are designed for the benefit of an entire neighborhood or other community. This chapter discusses programs that improve physical conditions, economic conditions, and social conditions in the community.

economic development: activities to create new jobs and additional sales and other business

A city worker cares for the grounds in Raleigh. Well-maintained parks beautify many North Carolina communities.

Governments can support community improvement in three ways: by delivering public service, by encouraging private action, and by regulating private behavior. In the public service approach to litter control, the government finds someone to pick up the litter. The government may encourage people to volunteer to pick up litter. For example, the North Carolina Department of Transportation's "Adopt a Highway" program encourages community organizations and businesses to pick up trash voluntarily along rural roads all across the state. The government may also assign its employees to pick up litter. A second way governments support community improvement is by encouraging private action. Governments encourage people not to throw trash away in public places. "Keep Our City Beautiful" campaigns are an example of this alternative. Finally, governments can regulate private behavior by making littering illegal and imposing fines on those who litter.

This chapter focuses on the first two approaches: public service and public encouragement of private action as ways to make the community better. Chapter 6 addresses government regulation of private behavior.

The Community's Physical Condition

Local governments often seek to change or protect the physical condition of their communities. To do this, local governments establish programs to protect people and property from natural hazards and pests, as well as programs to make their communities more attractive places to live and work.

In many places, local governments build and maintain drainage ditches or levees to help prevent flooding. Coastal towns have programs to replenish the sand on eroded beaches. Cities in the piedmont and mountains have programs to remove snow and ice from their streets. These services are typically carried out by the local government's public works department.

Counties throughout the state have programs to control mosquitoes, rats, stray dogs, and other

A plow removes snow from a street in Raleigh after the area received about a foot of snow.

potentially harmful animals. The county health department sprays for mosquitoes and poisons rats. Many local governments also have an animal control office. However, voluntary animal protection societies often contract with local government to operate shelters for dogs, cats, and other stray animals and to encourage responsible pet ownership.

Historic preservation programs identify and protect buildings and areas that have special significance in a community. These programs encourage pride in the community and its heritage. The programs also prevent old buildings and neighborhoods from becoming run-down and help renovate those that are run-down. Local governments support historic preservation in several ways. Many governments have sponsored building inventories to identify and describe buildings of historic or architectural interest. Publication of the inventory may encourage the owners of listed buildings to maintain them or even restore them to their original appearance.

Local governments can also provide incentives for maintaining and restoring historic buildings, such as making low-interest loans available. Banks or other local companies may also join with local government in

The Holly Avenue historic district in Winston-Salem is one of many in the state that is protected from becoming deteriorated.

support of historic preservation or other efforts to prevent the deterioration or to encourage the restoration of neighborhoods.

Sometimes buildings are in such poor condition that they are beyond repair and unsafe to use. Local governments can buy these buildings and demolish them to remove the hazard.

Government beautification programs include planting trees and flowers, and installing public art displays, flags, and holiday decorations. Efforts like these are often paid for by counties or municipalities and carried out by government employees. Sometimes, however, the government might hire a private company to do the work or assign the work to people who have been convicted of driving while intoxicated or other offenses.

Local governments also encourage garden clubs or civic organizations to help with community beautification and litter control. The general public can be encouraged to help, too. Campaigns publicize the benefits of an attractive community and urge people to "pick up, paint up, fix up." Contests to see who can pick up the most litter or produce the most beautiful flowerbeds provide a way to recognize

In the NEWS...

Kannapolis Citizens Weave a Shared Vision

By Eleanore J. Hajian

In 1998, Kannapolis leaders had a tough dilemma. They had to figure out how to inspire residents to participate in civic life and support their city government in a former mill town with a strong tradition of corporate paternalism.

Kannapolis had endured as the largest unincorporated city in the country (population nearly 30,000) until 1984. Prior to that, Cannon Mills provided water and sewer services, police and fire protection, roads and recreational amenities. The mill also maintained 1,600 company-owned homes and employed most of the town's residents. The corporate paternalism came to a screeching halt when the mill changed ownership in the early 80s, but its legacy continued. Two years ago that legacy began to change as city leaders began a visioning process that drew hundreds of residents.

Last month, that visioning process received the Program Excellence Award for Citizen Involvement at the International City/County Management Association conference in Cincinnati, OH. The award recognizes successful strategies designed to inform citizens about local government services and include them in the decision-making process. ICMA presented the award in the 50,000 and under population category to the city and to City Manager David Hales and Assistant City Manager Greg McGinnis.

Weaving A Shared Future, Kannapolis' 18-month visioning process held from May 1998 to October 1999, established a vision center on Main Street where citizens spent more than 1,000 volunteer hours sharing their memories, ideas and dreams for their city. More than 100 volunteers chaired and participated in committees designated as live, work, learn and play. The four committees were charged with finding solutions to the

A volunteer leads a group of 100 citizens at an all-day visioning session.

issues Kannapolis faced. The result: a strategic plan to strengthen neighborhoods, add recreational facilities and attract new business to the city.

But Kannapolis gained much more than a good plan, said McGinnis, who served as vision coordinator. "Prior to this visioning process a lot of our residents never really had the opportunity to have a say in what they want the town to be," he said. "It was a citizen-led process. When we had the final presentation of the plan at least 500 people came, and it got a standing ovation from the community."

It's an award the city can be proud of, said Mayor Ray Moss.

"Because of the hundreds of people who participated in Weaving a Shared Future, we have a vision that will carry us for the next 15 to 20 years and a strategic plan that comes directly from our people," he said. "What's really wonderful about this award is that it recognizes our citizens for their participation and our staff for their hard work."

—Excerpted with permission from *Southern City*, November 2000.

outstanding efforts. Often, much of the work to improve the physical condition of a community is done by **volunteers**—people who give their time and effort to making their neighborhoods safer and more attractive.

volunteers:
people who donate their time and effort

The Community's Economic Condition

Local governments are interested in attracting and keeping businesses in their communities because businesses provide jobs and pay taxes. The people in a community need jobs to earn income. Taxes paid by businesses can help reduce the taxes residents have to pay to support local government. For these reasons, many local governments seek to play an important part in shaping the community's economy.

Many cities and counties support economic development by helping fund the local **chamber of commerce.** Chambers of commerce provide information about communities to people who may be interested in doing business there. Links to local chamber of commerce Web sites for cities and counties throughout North Carolina are listed at http://www.edgecombe.cc.nc.us/CHAMBER/OTHERS.HTM

chamber of commerce:
a group of business people formed to promote business interests in the community

More than 60 North Carolina counties have formed economic development commissions to improve their local economies. Economic development commissions attract new industries and other businesses and support existing business and industry. The commissions collect information about the local economy and work force, advertise the advantages of their communities, and help businesses organize support they may need from local government and others. For example, the economic development commission may work with businesses, local schools, and community colleges to help the schools and colleges develop job training needed by the businesses. Or the economic development commission may work with a **business development corporation** to create an industrial park or to renew a downtown area.

business development corporation:
a group of people legally organized as a corporation to encourage economic development

Charlotte is planning to revitalize the area along Stonewall Street by building shops and housing.

In the NEWS...

North Carolina Cities Aim to Wipe Out Brownfields with EPA Grants

By Eleanore J. Hajian

The former Scotland Memorial Hospital Building in Laurinburg is one of those places cities and towns dread. It's abandoned. It's falling apart. It's overgrown with vegetation.

After 15 years of vandals, derelict owners, and Mother Nature taking their toll, the hospital has become what's called a brownfield—a place that no one wants to or can develop because of perceived or real contamination. In this case, asbestos is the likely suspect.

The old hospital is the chief plague of the residential neighborhood, elementary school and park it abuts, bringing crime and vagrants to an otherwise healthy area, said Mayor Ann Slaughter.

"It's the biggest eyesore I've ever seen," she said. "It's a nice neighborhood, but we've been left with that."

But there's now an end in sight for Laurinburg, which along with Concord received a Brownfield Assessment Demonstration Pilot grant from the U.S. Environmental Protection Agency to help evaluate the environmental contamination of brownfield sites.

Vice President Al Gore in May awarded more than $35 million in grants to 102 communities across the country to clean up brownfields and return them to economically thriving, community hubs. They included 56 Brownfields Assessment Pilot grants totaling more than $12 million.

The grants will provide Concord and Laurinburg $200,000 to assess brownfield properties and develop plans for fixing them up. Both cities also received $50,000 in grant funding exclusively to develop green spaces such as parks.

Receiving the grant offers new hope to towns like Laurinburg, said Slaughter.

"If the grant can help us to realize what can be done with the building, just knowing the possibilities will mean a great deal to the community and to those outside of the community," she said. "Just having the money to evaluate it and knowing what the real cost will be to someone who may be interested in developing it means a lot."

The city plans to use the grant money to assess other sites as well, including a burned [down] auto shop on Main Street, an abandoned gas station across from the local high school and several industrial and warehouse buildings near the railroad.

In Concord, officials plan to use the grant money to transform three city-owned brownfield sites—an electric utility warehouse, a garage and a motor park—into a thriving marketplace, a park with a greenway and a traditional neighborhood.

The former Scotland Memorial Hospital building in Laurinburg will be evaluated for possible re-use.

(Continued from page 62)

The grant funding will help Concord complete the first step toward the cleanup and redevelopment process, said Susie Zakraisek, a senior planner in community development.

Two other North Carolina cities will benefit from EPA brownfield funding. Winston-Salem and Fayetteville each received $500,000 from the Brownfields Cleanup Revolving Loan Fund pilot.

The grants will allow the cities to build on their past efforts by establishing revolving loan funds to provide businesses with low-interest loans for the cleanup and redevelopment of their brownfield sites.

Winston-Salem plans to use the money to help revitalize distressed business districts and Fayetteville will concentrate on redeveloping a 54-acre downtown area.

For more information on EPA brownfields programs, check out the following Internet site: www.epa.gov/brownfields/pilot.htm or call the EPA Region 4 Brownfields Team at (404) 562-8661.

—Reprinted with permission from *Southern City,* October 2000.

For example, in Fayetteville, city and county governments worked with a business development corporation called Fayetteville Progress to improve the city's downtown. Fayetteville Progress was formed by local business leaders to organize the downtown renewal. Fayetteville Progress coordinated the efforts of the City of Fayetteville and Cumberland County, various banks, and real estate developers to clear out some old buildings, to remodel others, and to build new offices, stores, and apartments. Asheville, New Bern, Raleigh, Wilmington, and many other cities and towns have also worked with private development corporations to improve their downtown areas.

Examples of special efforts that help make a community more attractive to businesses and industry include: preparing property for development by installing water lines, sewers, and roads; constructing buildings; offering low-interest loans; and coordinating job training with schools and colleges.

Groups of cities may also work together to encourage economic development. For example, more than 70 North Carolina cities that operate electric utilities have joined together in an association called ElectriCities. You can read about their economic development activities at http://www.electricities.com/

Because tourism is a major part of the economy in many parts of North Carolina, some cities and counties dedicate considerable efforts to make their communities more attractive to tourists. Tourism is especially important to the economy of the mountains, the coast, and the sandhills in the south central piedmont. In addition, all of the largest cities in the state actively seek to host conventions, adding another aspect to the tourism industry.

The 32 cities that belong to the North Carolina Association of Conventions and Visitors Bureaus sponsor a Web site (http://visit.nc.org/) and conduct other promotional activities to attract paying visitors to their communities. Many other towns and cities also have programs to attract tourists.

The Belle Chere Celebration in downtown Asheville is one way the city helps promote tourism.

Special efforts to promote tourism include festivals like Spivey's Corners' "Hollerin' Contest" and outdoor dramas like Boone's "Horn in the West." Advertising is important, too. Brochures and maps identify interesting places and events to entice visitors. Coliseums, stadiums, museums, and arts centers also help to attract tourists. Cities and counties support these places, in part at least, for the tourist business they generate.

Historic sites are major tourist attractions throughout North Carolina. One benefit of historic preservation programs is that they help develop and maintain areas of historic interest to tourists. Similarly, community beautification, recreation, and arts programs that local governments support for the benefit of their own residents frequently help attract tourists as well. These same features may also help attract new businesses and industries.

In addition, an abundant supply of safe water, adequate sewage-disposal capacity, good police and fire protection, good schools, and other public services that support a high quality of life are important to business and industry leaders who are looking for new locations for facilities. Thus, good "user-focused" services also contribute to economic development.

Social Relationships in the Community

Local governments also work to improve social relations in their communities. Some local governments have countywide or city-wide programs to promote understanding among different racial, ethnic, or religious groups and to encourage fair treatment of all people in the community. These efforts may be organized through a human relations commission. Another approach concentrates on improving relations among people in a particular neighborhood. Local governments support these efforts through community action agencies, through neighborhood or residents' associations, or even through police community-relations offices.

In North Carolina, most human relations commissions were established to improve race relations. Even today, relationships among North Carolinians of African, European, and Native American descent continue conflicts that began centuries ago. European settlers fought with Native Americans (whom the English colonists called "Indians") for control of the land. Some Europeans began to bring captive Africans here as slaves.

Myths about differences between the races and attitudes about European superiority that began during the Indian wars and during slavery continue to be learned and believed by many people. After the civil war, slavery was abolished and the former slaves became full citizens. African American North Carolinians participated actively in politics and were elected to state and local public offices, as well as to Congress. However, many whites in North Carolina continued to fear and look down on the former slaves (and on the few Native Americans still living in the state). In the late nineteenth century, a white majority in the General Assembly passed laws requiring segregation of the races. These minorities were denied basic civil rights, and government officials even overlooked violence against them. By 1900, few of North Carolina's African American or Native American citizens were able to vote or hold public office.

Not until the 1960s did African American and Native American North Carolinians regain their basic civil rights including the right to vote. Federal voting-rights laws ended **poll taxes** and other practices used to keep people from voting. Only then was segregation ended. Many white North Carolinians supported ending segregation and assuring civil rights for all North Carolinians. However, some whites continued to fear African Americans and Native Americans and to feel superior to them. At the same time, some African Americans and Native Americans continued to resent whites because of a long history of discrimination and mistreatment.

poll tax:
tax people had to pay in order to be allowed to vote

Human relations commissions were established primarily to find ways to ease racial tensions and to eliminate racial discrimination. The commissions hold public meetings to discuss potential problems among racial groups. Much of their work entails encouraging people of different races to talk and listen to one another. The commissions try to help people realize that cultural differences do not need to be threatening. The commissions also try to help people see the individuality of others whose race is different from their own. An important step in eliminating racism involves getting past stereotypes and recognizing a person as an individual.

Human relations commissions also deal with other problems of intolerance and discrimination based on race, ethnic group, religion, or gender. In recent years, new immigrants have come to North Carolina from Latin America and Asia. Sometimes they are the subject of discrimination or abuse by others who fear or resent them because of their race or origin.

Also, there are a growing variety of religious affiliations in North Carolina. Protestants remain the largest group, but there are also Catholics and people of other Christian denominations, Jews, Muslims, Buddhists, and other religious groups now living in the state. Human relations commissions try to help promote understanding of other religions and to prevent acts of religious discrimination.

A somewhat different social problem concerns relationships between women and men. Many deeply held attitudes about the

Police help encourage community cooperation by getting to know the residents and helping them work together to make their neighborhood a safer place.

roles of men and women developed when almost all women were married and worked full time at home. In recent years these social patterns have changed. Now most women work outside the home. Many women are single heads of households. Laws and social expectations about how men should treat women are changing. Married women now have the same property rights as their husbands, for example. Domestic violence is no longer treated as a "family" matter, but is now a crime of assault, which means the police and the courts are now responsible for domestic violence cases. Human relations commissions help set up ways for men and women who are concerned about these changes to communicate with each other in order to understand the issues and each other better.

Local governments may also work with residents of a neighborhood to help build trust and a sense of responsibility. Crime and other social problems are often greatest in areas where people do not trust their neighbors or do not believe that they can or should do anything for each other. Community Action Programs and other neighborhood-based programs help people work together on projects to benefit the neighborhood. Residents' councils can promote cooperation and improvement in public housing or help fight youth drug abuse.

Police can also encourage neighborhood cooperation. For example, Greensboro police set up Police Neighborhood Resource Centers in the city's public housing communities. Each of these police ministations has two officers who are permanently assigned there. The officers patrol the housing communities on foot and get to know the residents. In addition to criminal investigations and emergency response services, these officers help residents get the social services and health services they need. Some services are even provided right in the mini-station. The officers also organize recreation for neighborhood youth. As a result of the police officers' efforts, people have begun to trust each other and the police, increasing residents' willingness to report crimes, ask for police assistance, and assist the police. This increased cooperation with the police reduces crime and makes the neighborhoods safer for all the residents.

Deciding What to Do

People sometimes disagree about what local government should do to improve the community. One source of disagreement is differences about how much change is desirable. Some people might want more ditching or beach erosion-control devices, but others might want to limit human interference with natural

In the
NEWS...

Greenboro's Long-term Commitment to Affordable Housing Aids Families and Builds Strong Neighborhoods

By Eleanore Hajian

With a strong commitment to affordable housing and neighborhood development programs that goes back 50 years, Greensboro has seen the change such programs can make to a city or town, and the people who live there.

Since the city dedicated one cent of its property taxes to the effort, programs administered by the Greensboro's Housing and Community Development Department have helped thousands of low- and mid-income families buy homes for the first time and rehabilitate existing homes. City support has also helped several nonprofit agencies build thousands of affordable homes. Other department programs have helped renovate hundreds of apartments [and] historic homes and improve neighborhoods.

The nationally acclaimed efforts have enabled Greensboro to boast what few towns and cities can.

"This is a community with no real slums," said Andrew Scott, HCD director. "We have some really bad stuff here and there, but there's precious little of the bad slums you see in other places. We do not have a lot of the apparent problems other cities have."

The city's long-standing public policy emphasizing the need for strong neighborhoods and quality housing for all Greensboro residents, has made it possible to reinvest in and protect the city's housing stock, Scott said.

But the effort goes beyond providing physical structures, and so do the benefits the effort brings to the community, said Rhonda Enoch, a housing counselor who

During Project Homestead's second Housing Blitz, more than 400 volunteers worked three days on 50 homes. The Blitz helps meet the demand for homes under $85,000.

helps clients qualify and prepare for home ownership.

"This program has produced stability for families in this community and given them some sense of wealth," she said. "It makes the city a better place to live. You can live anywhere in the city limits and not feel that your family is in danger of losing life or property."

Owning a home can do a lot for a family, especially the children, Scott said.

"One of our clients said her son gets off the school bus differently now," he said. "People take more of an interest in things in neighborhoods where they own."

For many clients, the purchase of a home through HCD provides the boost they need to achieve financial stability and get ahead. A lot of times an HCD loan enables people to purchase homes earlier in their lives. Many clients have moved on to purchase bigger homes in later years. More older residents have been able to stay in their ailing homes because of housing rehabilitation assistance.

(Continued from page 67)

Another impact has been an increased willingness of Realtors and lenders to work a lower end market.

"They know that Rhonda is here, and they will work with people," Scott said. "Ninety-nine percent of the people who come through our door end up qualifying."

The bottom line is that because of Greensboro's housing and community development programs, more city residents have better lives, and that's a benefit that's hard to measure, Scott said.

"They are the kind of intangibles that it's hard to put a finger on, but you definitely see quality of life enhancements," he said.

—Reprinted with permission from *Southern City,* January 2001.

drainage or beach movement. Another source of disagreement concerns the relative importance of various public programs. Some people place high value on an attractive community and want to see public funds spent on improving community appearance. Others may argue that public funds should be spent on other public services that they consider more important. People might also have differing opinions about the kinds of new industry that government should encourage, or even whether additional economic development is good for their community. People might also have different views about desirable social relations in the community.

proposal:
a suggestion put forward for consideration or approval

Proposals for public programs to improve the community are usually presented long before any action is taken. Often, an initial discussion at a meeting of the city council or board of county commissioners introduces a proposal to both elected officials and the public. Proposals may be developed by the city or county manager, by other staff members, by appointed advisory boards, by elected officials, or by private citizens.

News reporters play an important role in spreading word of a new proposal to the public. Stories in newspapers or on the radio or television inform people in the community about the proposal. Groups of people with similar interests may also pay particular attention to the topics discussed by the governing board and alert their members when an issue of particular concern comes up. For example, the local real estate dealers' association and environmental protection groups like the Sierra Club might both be interested in a proposed change in drainage ditches, although for different reasons. The real estate agents might support the plan in order to protect buildings or to create more building sites. On the other hand, the environmental protection groups might oppose the plan because they fear it would harm wildlife or water quality.

People who favor or oppose a proposal can express their concerns about it in various ways. They may write letters to the editor of their local newspaper or give interviews to news reporters.

They may speak to friends and to members of groups with whom they share common interests. They may speak at public meetings or talk to the city or county manager or other staff members. Most importantly, however, they must communicate their concerns to members of the local government's governing board. The elected representatives on the governing board have the authority and the responsibility to decide whether or not to approve the proposal. People call or write their elected representatives and present **petitions** signed by many voters to express their opinions about a proposal. According to North Carolina's "Open Meetings Law," the governing board's meetings must be open to the public. Thus, reporters can cover the debates and publicize the arguments for and against proposed programs. **Proponents** and **opponents** can attend these meetings and express their opinions to elected officials.

Often, plans are changed to reflect the concerns of opponents while continuing to meet the most important objectives of the proponents. Sometimes, however, elected officials are unable or unwilling to adopt a program that pleases everyone. Opponents who feel strongly about the plan may continue to try to prevent it even after it has been adopted. They might file a lawsuit, asking the courts to stop work on the program. Or they might campaign against representatives who voted for the program, hoping to elect new members of the governing board who will vote to stop the program. Those who supported the proposal are likely to continue their interest in it and to go on backing the members of the board who voted for the plan.

Once a program has been authorized by the governing board, local government employees begin to carry it out. Many approaches to community betterment also require active public cooperation to succeed. The organized cooperation of businesses, community groups, schools, and other parts of the community is very important for many community improvement activities. Programs that are designed to encourage people to fix up their property, pick up litter, or work with their neighbors to improve community relations all depend on the people in a community for their success.

petition:
a request for government action signed by a number of voters who support the same request

proponent:
one who is in favor of something

opponent:
one who is against something

Discussion Questions

1. **What programs does your city or county have to improve its physical condition?**

2. **What programs does your city or county have to improve its economic condition?**

3. **What programs does your city or county have to improve its social condition?**

4. **How could you, your family, or your school help with these improvement programs?**

6

Regulating Harmful Behavior

O ne of the most powerful tools local governments have to improve their communities is the authority to regulate harmful behavior within their jurisdictions. North Carolina state law gives counties and municipalities authority to regulate various activities to protect people from harm. For example, local governments can pass "leash laws" requiring owners to control their dogs, thereby reducing the danger of people being bitten. Local governments can adopt building restrictions to prevent people from constructing buildings in areas that are likely to be flooded. City governments set speed limits and other regulations for traffic on city streets.

Who decides what behavior is likely to be harmful enough to need regulation? How are these decisions made? What kinds of behavior do North Carolina cities and counties frequently regulate? How do they enforce these regulations? This chapter will answer these questions.

crime:
an act that is forbidden by law; an offense against all of the people of the state, not just the victim of the act

Traffic laws help make streets safer by regulating how people drive. Cameras at stoplights are a relatively new approach to enforcing traffic laws.

Regulating Personal Behavior

Governments regulate personal behavior that threatens people's ability to live and work together in safety and security. Many of the laws against disruptive behavior are made by the state General Assembly. For example, state laws declare certain acts to be **crimes.** Crimes are offenses against all of the people of North Carolina, not just the victim who is harmed directly by the act. State laws also provide rules for the safe operation of cars and trucks on the state's highways. State laws apply to the entire state.

Local governments also have the responsibility to determine what kind of behavior they want to regulate within their jurisdictions. But there are limits to their authority to regulate. Local

Burning of household trash, prohibited by both state law and local ordinance, led to this fire in a Wadesboro neighborhood.

government regulations must not violate either the state or federal constitution, and local governments must have authority for their regulations from the state of North Carolina. Local governments in North Carolina have broad authority to regulate behavior that creates a public nuisance and threatens the public health, safety, or welfare. Other kinds of local regulation require special acts of authorization by the General Assembly.

Behavior that is acceptable in one community may be regulated as a nuisance in another community. For example, while some local governments have ordinances that require dog owners to keep their dogs penned or on a leash, some do not. Some cities and towns have ordinances regulating the loudness and/or the time of noisy behavior in residential areas. Some local governments prohibit burning trash or leaves. Views about the seriousness of the harm caused by an activity often vary from place to place across North Carolina.

Views about the harmfulness of an activity also change over time. For example, many cities and towns in North Carolina used to require stores to be closed all day on Sunday. Over the past 30 years, most of those ordinances have been repealed. In many parts of the state, more people wanted to shop on Sunday, and more merchants wanted to sell on Sunday. Fewer people believed it was wrong to conduct business on Sunday (or, even if they believed it was wrong, that the government should keep others from shopping on Sunday). Not everyone agreed, however. Often, as change occurs, some people continue to hold on to their old views of an activity, while others come to see its harmfulness quite differently.

Wadesboro Code

Chapter 94: Fire Prevention, Explosives; Fireworks
Fire Hazards § 94.01 Open burning; control and prohibitions.

No person shall cause, suffer, allow or permit open burning of refuse or other combustible material except as may be allowed in compliance with divisions (A) through (F) of this section, or except by a permit issued by the town, or by a permit issued by the North Carolina Board of Water and Air Resources. The following types of open burning are permissible as specified if burning is not prohibited by ordinances and regulations of governmental entities having jurisdiction. The authority to conduct open burning under the provision of this section does not exempt or excuse a person from the consequences, damages or injuries which may result from such conduct nor does it excuse or exempt any person from complying with all applicable laws, ordinances, regulations, and orders of the governmental entities having jurisdiction even though the open burning is conducted in compliance with this section:

(A) Fires purposely set for the instruction and training of public and industrial firefighting personnel.

(B) Fires purposely set to agricultural lands for disease and pest control and other accepted agricultural or wildlife management practices.

(C) Fires purposely set to forestlands for accepted forest management practices.

(D) Fires purposely set in rural areas for rights-of-way maintenance.

(E) Camp fires and fires used solely for outdoor cooking and other recreational purposes or for ceremonial occasions.

(F) The burning of trees, brush and other vegetable matter in the clearing of land or rights-of-way with the following limitations:

(1) Prevailing winds at the time of burning must be away from any city or town or built-up area, the ambient air for which may be significantly affected by smoke, fly-ash, or other air contaminants from the burning;

(2) The location of the burning must be at least 1000 feet from any dwelling located in a predominantly residential area other than a dwelling or structure located on the property on which the burning is conducted;

(3) The amount of dirt on the material being burned must be minimized;

(4) Heavy oils, asphaltic materials, items containing natural or synthetic rubber or any materials other than plant growth may not be burned;

(5) Initial burning may generally be commenced only between the hours of 9:00 A.M. and 3:00 P.M., and no combustible material may be added to the fire between 3:00 P.M. of one day and 9:00 A.M. of the following day, except that under favorable meteorological conditions deviations from the above-stated hours of burning may be granted by the air pollution control agency having jurisdiction. It shall be the responsibility of the owner or operator of the open burning operation to obtain written approval for burning during periods other than those specified above.

('76 Code, § 4.27) (Ord. passed 1-11-71) Penalty, see § 10.99

This is an example of a local ordinance in Wadesboro.

More recently there has been controversy as communities have begun to regulate smoking in public places. In this case, the old view was that smoking was not a public problem. In fact, the use of tobacco was even seen by some North Carolinians as a sort of patriotic duty. Tobacco was North Carolina's chief crop. Much of the state's economy depended on raising tobacco, wholesaling it, and manufacturing cigarettes and other tobacco products. This traditional view began to be challenged as medical researchers linked tobacco smoke to cancer, heart disease, and breathing disorders. Evidence that non-smokers' health could be negatively affected by breathing others' second-hand smoke has increased the conviction among many people that smoking tobacco in public places should be prohibited. And as fewer and fewer people in the United States smoke, tobacco has also become a smaller part of the state's economy.

The case of Greensboro provides a good illustration of how people participate in a local government's decision to regulate behavior. In June 1988, Greensboro resident Lori Faley presented the Greensboro City Council a petition asking the council to regulate smoking in public places. Ms. Faley started the petition after someone blew smoke in her face while she stood in a supermarket checkout lane. The petition she brought to the city council had more than 500 signatures and called for an ordinance regulating smoking in stores and restaurants, as well as in publicly owned buildings. There was immediate opposition to the ordinance, especially from tobacco companies and workers in Greensboro. (More than 2,300 people were employed in the tobacco industry there.) The city council held a public hearing on the request and then appointed a committee to study the issue. The committee was to be made up of representatives from the council, the county commission, the county health department, and business owners and managers, but it was slow to organize. It finally held its first meeting in July 1989.

Ms. Foley and her group, which became known as GASP (Greensboro Against Smoking Pollution), were frustrated at the council's response and did not wait for the study committee to meet. GASP began to collect signatures on another petition. This petition took advantage of a provision in the Greensboro Charter for procedures called **initiative** and **referendum.** (Greensboro is one of only a few North Carolina cities with provisions for initiative and referendum.)

The GASP petition called for the council to vote on the ordinance regulating smoking in public places. It also called for a referendum on the ordinance if the council failed to adopt it. The initiative petition required the valid signatures of 7,247 Greensboro voters to force a referendum.

In August 1989, GASP submitted its petition. Although more than 10,000 people had signed the petition, only 7,306 signatures were certified as those of registered Greensboro voters. Still, that

initiative:
a way in which the citizens propose laws by gathering voter signatures on a petition; only a few cities and no counties in North Carolina have provisions for this

referendum:
an election in which citizens vote directly on a public policy question

was more than the number necessary to require a vote. The council refused to adopt the ordinance, and the referendum was placed on the ballot for the November election.

Greensboro tobacco companies spent tens of thousands of dollars urging voters to defeat the ordinance. GASP did not have similar financial resources, but the group did have the names of those who had signed the petition. GASP members called those people to urge them to vote for the ordinance. The ordinance passed by a very narrow margin: 14,991 votes for and 14,818 against.

That did not end the controversy, however. Tobacco workers in Greensboro began an initiative petition of their own. This time, the petition called for a referendum to repeal the smoking regulation ordinance, which the voters adopted in 1989. The petitioners collected the required number of signatures, and another election was held in 1991. In this election, the result was the same. Voters rejected repealing the ordinance by more than two to one. Although thousands of people in Greensboro were still unhappy with the city's regulation of smoking in public places, Greensboro voters overwhelmingly supported keeping the ordinance.

Regulating the Use of Property

Local governments regulate the use of property to protect the physical environment, to encourage economic development, or to protect people's health and safety. Several different kinds of property regulations are commonly used.

In many jurisdictions, a land use plan serves as the basis for much of the regulation of property use. City or county planners (or outside consultants) study the physical characteristics of the land. (Where are the steep slopes? What areas are subject to flooding?) They map existing streets, rail lines, water lines, sewers, schools, parks, fire stations, and other facilities that can support development. They also note current uses of the land. (Where are the factories, the warehouses, the stores and offices, the residential neighborhoods?)

On the basis of their studies, the planners prepare maps showing how various areas might be developed to make use of existing public facilities and to avoid mixing incompatible uses (keeping factories and junkyards separate from houses, for instance). The maps may also indicate where new water lines and sewers might be built most easily. These maps are then presented to the public for comment. After the public has reviewed the maps, the planners prepare a detailed set of maps showing current and possible future uses of the land. The local governing board may review and vote on this final set of maps itself or delegate planning authority to an appointed planning board. The approved maps and supporting narrative become the official land use plan for the community, called a Comprehensive Plan.

All except the smallest North Carolina cities and towns have land use plans. Municipal land use plans typically cover an area

Johnston Towns Want to be Able to Control Their Space

By Adrienne Lu

There's friction brewing in Johnston County over who should control the land around town borders.

Many towns are concerned that the county allows too much suburban sprawl. They want control over more of the land just outside town limits so the sprawl doesn't creep near them—and into areas that eventually could be annexed. But county commissioners aren't leaping at the chance to give up authority.

Whoever wins the argument will get a huge say in Johnston County's future. Will the towns' visions of orderly development around their borders prevail? Or will the county continue to allow development more suited to rural life on the edge of town limits?

Four Oaks has struggled with the county more than once over such issues. Over the past year, four duplexes have popped up on a bare patch of dirt off Black Creek Road, a stone's throw from Four Oaks' planning jurisdiction.

Linwood Parker, a Four Oaks commissioner, said that if the town had had a say in how the duplexes were built, the area would look very different. In all likelihood, Four Oaks would have required landscaping, paved roads and a parking lot, Parker said. "The county didn't do us right in this situation," Parker said.

James H. Langdon, Jr., chairman of the county commissioners, doesn't understand why Four Oaks doesn't like the duplexes, which meet county standards. "Now they keep telling us they're terrible," Langdon said. "I reckon it's an opinion."

Technically, the debate is whether towns should be allowed to expand their extraterritorial jurisdictions—the areas outside town limits where towns have planning and zoning control. The state established extraterritorial jurisdictions decades ago as a way to give towns control over development just outside town limits that could affect the town and over areas that eventually could be annexed.

What's really at stake, though, is who gets to decide how growth happens around towns.

Town officials say the county hasn't done a great job handling all the growth in the county. Some say the area around Interstate 40 and NC 42 was a huge planning mistake by the county, with its traffic tie-ups and dangerous intersections.

The county commissioners haven't said they won't approve extraterritorial jurisdiction expansion requests. But it's clear also that the county won't approve them freely. Most people don't like the idea of living in extraterritorial jurisdictions, where they don't pay town taxes, receive town services or vote for town officials, but must abide by town zoning and development rules. The county doesn't want to anger those who would be affected.

"My position is on one simple [criterion]," county commissioner Tom Moore said. "Is it good for the town? Is it good for the people they're going to take in it? And is it good for the county? You justify that, even two out of three, and I will consider it. But without any reason, justification, no."

The towns say their requests are justified. "We want to be sure that the town controls its own destiny," said Skip Browder, planning director and assistant town manager for Clayton.

For now, the county has asked the towns to come up with a list of criteria on which the county should judge requests; it could be months before any real decisions are made.

—Excerpted with permission from
The News & Observer, Raleigh, North Carolina,
November 18, 2000.

extraterritorial land use planning jurisdiction:
the area outside city limits over which a city has authority for planning and regulating use

zoning:
rules designating different areas of land for different uses

subdivision regulation:
rules for dividing land for development

one mile beyond the municipal boundaries. The area outside the city limits, but under the city's planning authority, is called the **extraterritorial land use planning jurisdiction.** With the approval of the county commissioners, a city may extend its extraterritorial land use planning jurisdiction even farther.

Counties have authority to regulate land use only over the parts of the county not subject to city planning. Because of cities' extraterritorial jurisdiction for land use planning, the county land use planning area is even smaller than the unincorporated area of the county. By 1997 a total of 63 North Carolina counties had adopted land use plans. Another 20 counties had developed plans, but these had not been formally adopted by the Board of County Commissioners.

Local officials can also use land use plans to guide their decisions about where to locate new public facilities. Some governments use them only for these non-regulatory purposes. A land use plan also establishes a basis for regulation of property uses. However, the plan itself does not set up a system of regulation. **Zoning** and **subdivision regulations** are systems of regulation based on a land use plan.

Zoning

Zoning sets up restrictions on the use of land. The local governing board establishes categories of land use. Then the categories are applied to specific areas of the jurisdiction, creating zones for different kinds of development. The categories specify the kinds of activities the land can and cannot be used for and various requirements for developing and using the land. For example, one residential category might be for single-family homes. That category might prohibit any apartments, office buildings, or industrial centers in the zone. It might also require that each lot be a minimum size and that buildings be constructed a specified distance from the boundaries of the lot and at a maximum building height. Another zoning category might be commercial. It might prohibit industrial activity in the zone and require a certain number of parking spaces be built for every 1,000 square feet of commercial floor space built. Districts allowing mixed use developments such as apartments, offices, and low intensity business uses that are compatible in the same area can also be regulated by the zoning code.

To develop property that has been zoned, the builder must obtain a zoning certificate from the planning department. The planning department staff checks the building plans for the property to see that all zoning requirements are met. The department then issues a zoning certificate. The Building Department can then issue a building permit to allow construction to begin if the building plans conform to the local and state building code. As building proceeds, inspectors check to see that construction meets the requirements of the state building code. The building code sets standards for safe construction, including plumbing and electrical systems. Inspectors

Sample Zoning District Map

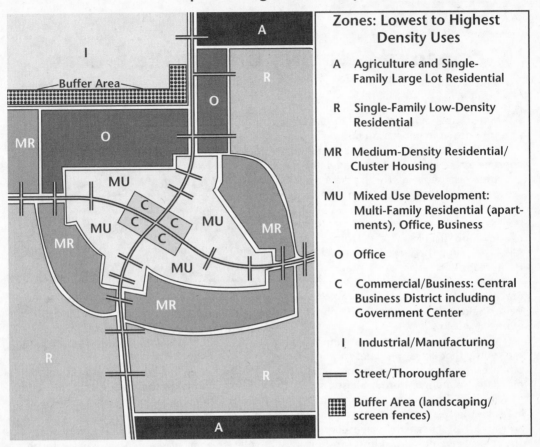

Zones: Lowest to Highest Density Uses

A Agriculture and Single-Family Large Lot Residential

R Single-Family Low-Density Residential

MR Medium-Density Residential/ Cluster Housing

MU Mixed Use Development: Multi-Family Residential (apartments), Office, Business

O Office

C Commercial/Business: Central Business District including Government Center

I Industrial/Manufacturing

══ Street/Thoroughfare

▦ Buffer Area (landscaping/ screen fences)

also check to make sure the zoning requirements are being followed. Before the new building can be occupied, inspectors must certify that it meets all state and local requirements, including the zoning regulations. An occupancy permit is then issued.

Zoning applies to both existing and new uses of property. For example, an existing store in an area zoned residential would not be forced to close if it was constructed before the zoning took effect. It would be considered a legal non-conforming use. However, expanding the store or changing its use to a factory might be prohibited by the zoning ordinance.

Minor exceptions to the zoning regulations can be made by the board of adjustment. This board is appointed by the council or commission. Boards of adjustment for cities with extraterritorial planning jurisdictions must include representatives from that area. The board of adjustment hears appeals about the decisions of the planning staff. It also hears requests for exceptions to the zoning regulations, called **variances.** Board of adjustment decisions usually cannot be appealed to the local governing board. Instead, appeals are made to the courts. This procedure is intended to keep political pressures from influencing land use decisions.

variance:
permission to do something that is different from what is allowed by current regulations

Speedway, county may strike a deal

By Erica Beshears

Racing will likely return to Tri-County Motor Speedway this spring after it abruptly closed in midseason last year.

The Caldwell County Commissioners must approve a race and practice schedule before activities can begin at the track. A vote is scheduled for March 18, County Manager Bobby White said.

This year, the track will be operated by its owner—Bob Brooks of the United Speed Alliance Racing, the sanctioning body for the Hooters ProCup series.

"We're going to operate the racetrack ourselves," the new track manager Jimmy Wilson said. "All of this has come about just in recent weeks."

The USAR will abide by an agreement with the county that limits the times for races and practices, requires mufflers for race cars and mandates sound-monitoring, Wilson said.

Wilson said he hopes the agreement will improve the relationship between the track and area residents, who have complained about excessive noise, dirt and irresponsible management since the track opened in 1985.

"We're going to do everything by the county's requirements," Wilson said. "The biggest thing is making the speedway to where it's a part of the community. There's been some tension (in the past.)"

Tri-County, a .4-mile oval in the Baton community, was built in a residential area before there was countywide zoning. Ever since, residents, county officials and the track have been at odds over track noise.

The commissioners require the track to submit a race and practice schedule for them to approve each year. Through the years, the different sides have reached agreements on decibel levels and mufflers, only to see them slowly unravel when the track changed owners or managers.

Last summer, the county put together a written record of all the agreements and requirements that had been discussed through the years.

County regulations helped solve a dispute between the owners of Tri-County Motor Speedway and neighbors of the speedway.

Soon after, the track abruptly closed. The people managing the track at that time cited the poor economy and unemployment as a reason for closing.

But the county used that compilation of rules for the agreement it is now forging with the USAR, commissioner John Thuss said.

"We have been through some less-than-wonderful relationships," Thuss said. "That makes it particularly difficult for (the new group) to pick up the pieces and move on . . . (But) I like their attitude."

According to the proposed schedule given to commissioners for consideration, the USAR would host 12 Friday nights of racing this year, from April 5 to August 16. Practice would be limited to Thursday between 5 P.M. and 7 P.M. On most race nights, practice and qualifying would begin at 5 P.M., and races would end by 11 P.M. For the three UARA shows, practice would begin at 4 P.M., and races would end by 11 P.M.

If the races run behind schedule, they will end no later than 11:30 P.M., Wilson said. "You really should be done racing by 11:30 P.M.," he said.

(Continued from page 78)

Each race car will have to have a muffler. And the track will check the decibel level of each car in an inspection before it can race, Thuss said. Each car's noise will have to be below 95 decibels measured at 100 feet, he said.

Thuss said he hoped the voluntary agreement keeps the track and local residents happy. If it doesn't work, the commissioners might investigate stricter special-use zoning options.

"They have certain rights," Thuss said of the track management. He said he has urged them to speak with the Baton community-planning group, to help build a relationship between the track and the community. "These folks genuinely do seem to be trying to be respectable managers and owners. That's what I'm counting on more than anything."

—Reprinted with permission from
The Charlotte Observer, March 10, 2002.
© *The Charlotte Observer*

Because major land use and zoning decisions can affect property values, traffic levels, noise levels, and many other aspects of life in a community, they are frequently controversial. To ensure opportunities for public discussion, all zone change requests require public hearings. Also, major developments such as shopping centers require "special-use permits" which can be granted only after a formal public hearing on the project.

All of North Carolina's larger cities and towns have zoning regulations that the city council has adopted by ordinance. A municipality's zoning authority also covers the extraterritorial planning jurisdiction, as well as the area within the municipality. Almost two-thirds of the counties also have zoning for at least some of their area not under municipal jurisdiction. Most of the areas of North Carolina which are not covered by zoning regulations are primarily agricultural, although popular resistance to having local government regulate land use has also prevented the adoption of zoning in some counties where there is considerable industry.

Subdivision Regulation

Subdivision regulation establishes a process for reviewing a landowner's request to divide a piece of land into building lots. With subdivision regulation, the local government will not approve dividing land into lots for houses until the landowner satisfies certain conditions. These conditions typically include building adequate streets and providing appropriate drainage. The conditions might also include laying water and sewer lines, if the new development is to be served by public water supply and sewers. In addition, each lot must be checked to see that it includes a safe building site. The landowner may also be asked to donate land for a park or **greenspace.** If land is subject to subdivision regulation by local government, the register of deeds cannot record the boundaries of the new lots without approval of the local government. This assures that all regulations are followed.

greenspace:
an area that is kept undeveloped to provide more open land in or near a city

Zoning can be controversial because not everyone agrees on how land should be used.

Subdivision regulation is intended to prevent developments on land that cannot support them (because it floods, for example, or because the soil does not allow septic tanks and no sewers were provided). Subdivision regulation is intended to ensure that adequate streets and drainage are provided by the **developer,** so that residents (or the local government) are not left with the expense of building adequate roads or drains. Because many of these problems developed in earlier subdivisions, subdivision regulation is being used more and more. Still, in 1992, more than a third of North Carolina counties had not adopted subdivision regulations. These were mostly rural counties where little development was occurring.

developer:
a person or business that builds houses or prepares land for building

Minimum Housing Codes

Minimum housing codes establish basic requirements for a place to be "fit for human habitation"—that is, acceptable as someone's living place. Typical requirements include structural soundness (to prevent the collapse of walls or floors), adequate ventilation (to provide the occupants with fresh air), and a safe water supply and toilet facilities (to prevent the spread of disease). If an inspector finds that a building does not meet minimum standards, the inspector can order it to be repaired or closed. A local governing board can adopt an ordinance ordering that a building which is beyond repair be demolished. Most of North Carolina's larger cities and counties have minimum housing codes.

Other Regulations

Other regulations also help protect the physical environment. Local governing boards may regulate community appearance. For example, they can prohibit signs they decide are too large or disturbing. They can regulate changes to the outside appearance of buildings in historic districts. Local governing boards can also protect fragile environments. For example, they may regulate

In the
NEWS...

Rolesville Faces Pain of "Progress"

By Kristin Collins

It was not the usual agenda for a Board of Commissioners meeting in this tiny town: People were sniffling into tissues, talking of heart attacks and nervous breakdowns.

All these new houses—shoehorned one on top of the other, right in their backyards— were going to ruin the neighborhood, they told the board.

"My wife has been so upset, she about had a nervous breakdown," a teary-eyed Larry Roper told the board. "My neighbor about had a heart attack."

The cause of the furor? A plan for 22 homes on half-acre lots, which will start going up any day. With that subdivision came the first painful pangs of growth in Rolesville, Wake County's smallest town.

People in much of Wake County got used to these kinds of things long ago. These days, lots of people would kill for houses on half-acre lots next door. They're fighting giant drugstores, hotels and apartment complexes.

But in this town of 900, half-acre lots sound to some like New York City. Rolesville hadn't seen strife like this since the early '90s, when it put in a sewer system.

Back then, remembers Mayor Joe Winfree, people were afraid that a sewer system would bring new houses and new people. They thought it would change the town they loved. Now, their predictions are starting to come true.

Those 22 homes—which are dubbed Brandiwood and will fill an undeveloped doughnut hole in Al's Acres—are only the beginning. Developers just broke ground on the town's first office building. They're carving roads for 20 more homes in another subdivision. And the town manager is negotiating with a developer who could bring 500 new homes to the south edge of town.

That shouldn't be news to people in Rolesville. A committee, made up of officials and residents, completed a long-range plan in 1999 that estimated the town would grow to 12,000 by 2025.

But it's a different matter when that growth starts appearing in people's backyards. And it's not taken lightly in a place that has long been a retreat from the bustle of the Triangle's growth.

Residents of many of the 31 homes in Al's Acres say they feel ignored by the town, trampled on by the developer. And many won't speak to the man who sold the land to a developer, Rolesville Fire Chief Rodney Privette, even though several residents go to church with his family.

Privette harbors a few hard feelings of his own. "I was born and raised here," he said. "They come in and buy an acre and think they own everything."

Developer Rick Grote, of Raleigh, said he finally stopped getting calls at home from the residents of Al's Acres, accusing him of such offenses as dumping brush behind their houses. But he said he is still shocked at the emotional outburst his small project caused, especially considering that the property was zoned to allow two houses an acre long before he bought it.

The mayor and board members spent hours with the concerned residents in Al's Acres. They persuaded Grote to improve drainage and cut one house from his plan— even though the original plan met town standards.

"We've not grown so large that we just make rules and say, 'Well, he followed the rules, so everything's fine,'" Commissioner Frank Hodge said.

Hodge and Mayor Winfree said they'll spend the time it takes to make growth as painless as possible for residents. Plus they pointed out, hopefully, the town doesn't have any more undeveloped sites sitting smack in the middle of established subdivisions.

—Excerpted with permission from *The News & Observer*, Raleigh, North Carolina, November 13, 2000.

Local and state officials had to approve a thoroughfare plan for this highway.

activities that cause soil erosion or regulate building in flood plains or in reservoir watersheds. Like most land use regulations, ordinances regulating community appearance and environmental protection are usually enforced by building inspectors or by the planning staff.

Local governments also regulate the ways people use public property. They frequently adopt ordinances setting up rules for the use of parks or other facilities open to the public. Cities and towns regulate traffic on their streets. For major thoroughfares (streets that carry traffic into and out of the city) the city or town shares this authority with the state. The city council itself can decide to put up stop signs or traffic signals or to set speed limits on most city streets, but not on some of the busiest. The city council must request state action to regulate traffic on thoroughfares. Because all rural public roads are the state's responsibility, county governments must ask for state action to control traffic in unincorporated areas. Local and state officials must both approve a thoroughfare plan for all major streets and highways.

New Issues in Regulation: Hog Farming

Local government regulation can be very controversial. During the 1990s, for example, North Carolina became one of the United States' leading producers of pork through the expansion of systems in which many farmers each raise thousands of pigs on contract with the packing companies that prepare the meat for market. To raise such large numbers of hogs, farmers keep them in barns, rather than letting them run outside. Some people wanted to regulate these large-scale hog farms because of problems created by the wastes the hogs produce. Because a great many hogs are confined in a small space, they produce large quantities of manure. The wastes are regularly washed out of the barns and pumped into open lagoons, where some of the liquids can evaporate. Hog waste is also a valuable fertilizer, so the material from the lagoons is often sprayed onto fields where crops are grown. People who live near the hog farms object to the smell from the hog waste, which can be quite intense. Some also complain that their wells are polluted by hog waste. Streams and rivers have also been polluted when lagoons leak or overflow following storms. These high concentrations of hog waste have killed fish and polluted drinking water downstream.

Several counties have tried to impose stricter requirements on hog farms than those set by the state. For example, in 1997 the Chatham County Board of Commissioners passed an ordinance requiring farmers to pay a deposit into a fund the county created to pay for cleaning up spills from hog lagoons. They also required more space between hog barns and other buildings where people live or work. Hog farmers challenged the Chatham County regulations in court.

The North Carolina Court of Appeals ruled that the county had no right to pass rules that are stricter than those set by the state.

In 2001 the Chatham County Board of Commissioners appealed the decision, asking the state Supreme Court to review the ruling of the Court of Appeals. Residents of Chatham County, and even the commissioners, themselves, are divided on the issue. Some see the hog farms as an important part of the county's economy. Others think the smell from the farms is a serious public nuisance and the threat of leaks from the lagoons is a major environmental hazard. You can explore this controversy further at http://checc.sph.unc.edu/rooms/library/hogs/index.htm, a Web site maintained by the School of Public Health of the University of North Carolina at Chapel Hill.

This aerial view shows a typical hog farm in North Carolina with multiple barns, waste lagoons, and spray fields.

Using the Authority to Regulate

To regulate an activity, the local governing board must first gain the appropriate authority from the state. Local governments have been given authority to regulate many kinds of behavior. If state law does not already permit local government regulation of an activity, local officials must ask the General Assembly to pass a bill granting that authority. Next, the local governing board must adopt an ordinance. The ordinance is a legal description by the board of the behavior that is being regulated and the actions the government will take against people who do not follow the regulation.

Frequently people disagree about whether a particular activity is harmful enough to require regulation. Local governing boards often hold public hearings to encourage full discussion of the arguments for and against a proposal to regulate. Sometimes an advisory board or a committee of residents also reviews the arguments about a proposed regulation and presents these to the governing board. People also often speak directly to board members about proposed regulations they particularly favor or oppose. However, the decision to regulate must be made by the local governing board. Unless a majority of the board thinks regulation is appropriate, no action will be taken. Except for a few cities (like Greensboro) that have initiative and referendum, an ordinance can be adopted only by the board.

Governments regulate either by requiring certain actions or by prohibiting certain actions. If someone fails to act according to the requirements of the ordinance, the government can either refuse them certain public services or impose penalties on them. The ordinance specifies what service may be withheld or what penalties may be imposed. Some regulations are enforced by withholding public services until the person acts as the regulation requires. For

One way local government regulation helps make the community safer is by requiring that construction is in compliance with building codes.

civil:
concerns government's role in relations among citizens

citation:
an official summons to appear before a court to answer a charge of violating a government regulation

example, a person who wants to connect his or her home to the public water supply must get permission from the water department. To protect the water supply, local regulations specify the kind of plumbing the owner must install. Then, before the water department turns on the water, an inspector checks the plumbing to be sure it meets specifications.

Frequently, people who violate an ordinance must pay a **civil** penalty of a specified amount of money. When an official enforcing the ordinance determines that a violation has occurred, the official issues a **citation** to the violator, assessing the civil penalty. Sometimes there are other penalties, too. For example, the ordinance regulating parking may include a provision for towing cars parked in parking places reserved for the handicapped. Violations of some ordinances may also carry a fine or time in the county jail. People charged with violating these ordinances have a hearing at which a magistrate or district court judge determines whether they are guilty of the violation and, if so, what their sentence will be.

Police officers are given responsibility for enforcing many local ordinances, but other local officials are also responsible for enforcing specific ordinances. These include fire inspectors, housing inspectors, and zoning inspectors. Often these same local officials are also responsible for enforcing state laws and regulations. Local police enforce North Carolina's criminal laws, as well as local ordinances. Local fire inspectors enforce the state fire-prevention code in addition to any local fire-prevention code. Local ordinances must not conflict with state laws and regulations.

Many regulations require popular support to achieve their purposes. For example, most people must cooperate with restrictions on smoking in public places or requirements to keep dogs under control in order for these ordinances to be effective. Police enforcement can help make people aware of the law, but the police cannot be everywhere at once and cannot deal with widespread violations of such ordinances. Fortunately, most people accept their responsibility to obey laws, even when they disagree with them. This is the basis for the success of most government regulations.

Discussion Questions

1. Are there any controversies over regulation of personal behavior or land use in your city or county?

   If so, find out as much as you can about the arguments for and against the regulation. What arguments are most convincing to you? Why?

2. Who will decide whether or not to adopt and enforce this controversial regulation?

   What do you expect them to decide to do? Why?

3. Schools have their own rules to regulate disruptive behavior. What are some of these rules at your school?

   What sorts of harm does each protect against?

7 Paying for Local Government

Local government services and programs cost money. Cities and counties have to pay the people who work for them. Local governments must also provide the buildings, equipment, and supplies for conducting public business. They must pay for public services they buy from businesses or community groups. In North Carolina, local government services and programs cost billions of dollars each year. In 2001 North Carolina county governments spent more than $9.3 billion, and North Carolina cities and towns spent almost $6.9 billion to provide services for the people of North Carolina. Within limits set by the state, local officials are responsible for deciding what to spend for local government and how to raise the money to cover those expenses.

A budget is a plan for raising and spending money. North Carolina law requires each city and each county to adopt an annual budget every year, including planned expenditures and **revenues** for the following year.

revenue: the income that a government collects for public use

The State of North Carolina sets very strict requirements that local governments must follow in managing their money. This was not always so. During the 1920s, many cities and counties in the state borrowed heavily. When the stock market crashed in 1929 and thousands of people lost their jobs, many local governments went even more heavily into debt. By 1931 the state's local governments were spending half of their property tax revenues each year on debt payments. More than half of the state's cities and counties were unable to pay their debts at some time during the Great Depression of the 1930s.

To restore sound money management to local government, the General Assembly created the North Carolina Local Government Commission and passed a series of laws regulating local government budgeting and finance. The Local Government Commission enforces

Local governments have to adopt a budget every year in order to pay for services such as waste removal.

those laws and with the Institute of Government of the University of North Carolina at Chapel Hill provides training and advice to local government budget and finance officers.

State regulation provides a strong framework for sound money management. But local officials still have primary responsibility for using city and county funds wisely and well. During the past 50 years, North Carolina local governments have established a national reputation for managing public money carefully and providing the public with good value for their dollars.

Budgeting

In North Carolina, local government budgets must be balanced. That is, the budget must indicate that the local government will have enough money during the year to pay for all the budgeted **expenditures.** Expenditures can be paid either from money received during the year (revenue) or from money already on hand at the beginning of the year **(fund balance).** A balanced budget can be represented by the following equation:

Expenditures = Revenues + Fund Balance Withdrawals

Thus, if a local government plans to spend $1 million, it must have a total of $1 million in revenues and fund balance. If it plans to raise only $900,000 in revenue, it needs to be able to withdraw $100,000 from the fund balance. If it plans to raise $950,000, it will need to draw only $50,000 from the fund balance.

The fund balance is like the local government's savings account. It helps the government deal with unexpected situations. Local government revenues are discussed later in the chapter. However, it is important to note here that the budget is based on revenue estimates—educated guesses about how much money the city or county will receive during the coming year. To be safe, local officials usually plan to spend nothing from the fund balance. That is, they budget expenditures equal to estimated revenues. Then if actual revenues are less than expected, they can withdraw from the fund balance to make up the difference. If revenues exceed actual expenditures, the money is added to the fund balance. If a government regularly withdraws from its fund balance, it will eventually use all of its savings and have no "rainy day" money left.

Deciding What to Spend

In North Carolina, annual budgets run from July 1 of one calendar year to June 30 of the following calendar year. This period is called the government's **fiscal year** because it is the year used in accounting for money. (*Fisc* is an old word for treasury.) "Fiscal year" is often abbreviated "FY." FY 2002, for example, means the fiscal year from July 1, 2001, to June 30, 2002. Each year the local governing board must adopt the annual budget before the new fiscal year begins on July 1.

expenditures:
money spent

fund balance:
money a government has not spent at the end of the year

fiscal year:
the 12-month period that may not coincide with the calendar year used by the government for record keeping, budgeting, taxing, and other aspects of financial management

Several months before the fiscal year begins, each local government department estimates how much more or less their services will cost in the coming year. For example, if a solid waste collection department is going to continue collecting the same amount of waste from the same number of places at the same frequency, its costs will be about the same. Fuel for the trucks may cost a little more, but if services do not change, next year's expenditures should be similar to this year's expenditures.

If, in the previous example, the city council decides to reduce the number of trash collections from twice a week to once a week, the department can reduce the number of employees and the number of miles driven by the trucks. The department will pay less in salaries and fuel bills and perhaps not have to buy replacement trucks as often. The change in services will therefore reduce estimated expenditures for the department.

On the other hand, if the city plans to annex several neighborhoods, the department may need to add trucks and crews to collect solid waste there. These new expenses for additional service will add to estimated expenditures for the department.

After department heads determine how much they think they will need for the next fiscal year, they discuss these estimates with the manager. The manager also looks at expected changes in the other expenditures. For example, employees' salaries will have to be increased in order for the local government to stay competitive with private employers. In addition to department requests, the manager must add these increases to the projected expenditures.

At the same time, the manager also prepares revenue estimates for the coming year. After all the estimates for both expenditures and revenues are complete, the manager compares the totals. If estimated revenues exceed estimated expenditures, the manager may recommend lowering local tax rates, adding to the fund balance, or beginning new programs and services. If estimated expenditures exceed revenues, the manager may recommend cutting expenditures, raising taxes or fees, or making withdrawals from the fund balance. It is the manager's responsibility to propose a balanced budget to the governing board.

The proposed budget lists the amount of money each department will spend in the coming year. It also lists the amount of money expected from each revenue source for the coming year and the amount the manager proposes to withdraw from (or add to) the fund balance.

The governing board reviews the proposed budget. With the proposed budget is information about the current year's budget, expenditures, and revenues. Council members and commissioners usually pay particularly close attention to proposed changes in spending to decide whether the services their government provides are the best use of public funds. They also pay careful attention to proposals to raise tax rates or the fees people pay for services.

Before the governing board adopts the budget, it must hold a public hearing. This provides people in the community an opportunity to express their views about the proposed budget. At any point in its review, the board can change the proposed budget. The annual budget must be adopted by a majority of the board.

Spending Public Funds

appropriate:
to assign government funds to a particular purpose or use

In adopting the budget, the governing board **appropriates** the expenditures. That is, the board authorizes the amount to be spent for each department during the coming fiscal year. The finance officer keeps records of all expenditures. Before each bill is paid during the year, the finance officer checks to see that there is enough money left in the department's appropriation to pay that bill. Expenditure records also help the manager coordinate government operations and help in planning the next year's budget. If the government needs to spend more than the amount listed in the budget for a particular purpose, the council (or commission) must pass a budget amendment.

Each local government's budget reflects the choice of services the local governing board has made. Local government budgets also reflect the way the General Assembly has allocated service responsibilities. Most municipalities spend much of their money on utilities, public safety, and streets. Most counties spend a majority of their money on education and human services.

The following circle graphs show how North Carolina local governments spent their money in the 2000–2001 fiscal year. (The most

Total Expenditures of North Carolina's Municipalities: Fiscal Year 2000–2001

Total expenditures $6,880,523,858

Utilities: (37%) water, sewer, electric, and gas services operated by municipal governments

Debt Service: (10%) both principal and interest

Streets/Transportation: (11%) street construction and repair, traffic signals, buses, and airports

General Government: (7%) central administration and support for all municipal services

Public Safety: (18%) police, fire, emergency communications, emergency medical services, animal control, and building inspections

Other: (17%) economic development; parks, recreation and other cultural programs; environmental protection; and so on

Other 17%
Public safety 18%
Utilities 37%
General government 7%
Streets/transportation 11%
Debt service 10%

Source: North Carolina Department of the State Treasurer

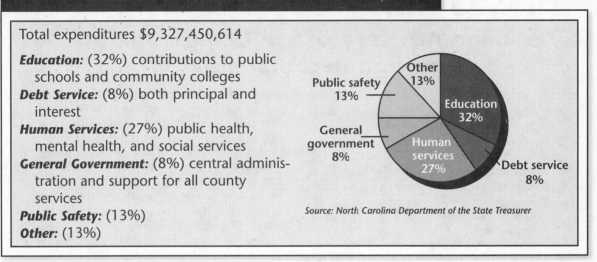

Total Expenditures of North Carolina's Counties: 2000–2001 Fiscal Year

Total expenditures $9,327,450,614

Education: (32%) contributions to public schools and community colleges

Debt Service: (8%) both principal and interest

Human Services: (27%) public health, mental health, and social services

General Government: (8%) central administration and support for all county services

Public Safety: (13%)

Other: (13%)

Other 13%
Public safety 13%
General government 8%
Education 32%
Human services 27%
Debt service 8%

Source: North Carolina Department of the State Treasurer

recent figures and additional detail can be found on the state treasurer's web site at http://ncdst-web2.treasurer.state.nc.us/lgc/units/unitlistjs.htm)

Local governments that borrow money to build new facilities must repay what they have borrowed—the **principal**—plus **interest.** Typically, these payments are spread over several years. These payments are called **debt service.** Debt service is often part of local government budgets, for reasons discussed in the following section.

Capital Projects

When a city buys land for a new park or a county builds a new jail or landfill, the project usually costs too much to be paid for from current revenues or from fund balance. Major purchases like land or buildings are called **capital** projects. Local governments usually borrow money to finance large capital projects, although annual revenues or fund balance may be sufficient for small projects.

Borrowing has several disadvantages. Borrowing money is expensive. The borrower (in this case, the city or county) must pay interest to the lender. Borrowing also commits the government to payments on the debt for a period of years, often 20 or more. Debt service payments will need to be included as expenses in each annual budget until the debt is paid off.

However, borrowing for capital projects also has advantages. One advantage is that by borrowing, the government can do the project right away. A new landfill or jail may be needed very soon—much sooner than the government would be able to save enough money to pay for the project. Another advantage to starting the project right away is that the costs of land and construction

principal:
the amount of money borrowed

interest:
a charge for borrowed money that the borrower agrees to pay the lender

debt service:
payments of principal and interest on a loan

capital:
previously manufactured goods used to make other goods and services; local governments' capital includes land, buildings, equipment, water and sewer lines, city streets and bridges

In the
NEWS...
Bond Advisory Group Begins Sorting Through Recommendations

By Virginia Knapp

It doesn't have dashing good looks or [charm], but it's guaranteed to be fought over and possibly attacked. Call it bond, county bond.

The Capital Needs Advisory Task Force meets to start the process of putting about $72 million in bonds before Orange County voters in November for a thumbs-up or thumbs-down.

The Orange County commissioners have charged the 28-member task force with recommending where funds should go and how much should be placed on the ballot.

"It's not just people bringing their own opinions, but it is also people listening to the community at large," task force member Bill Waddell said about the process of determining needs.

A sample scenario for the November bond referendum suggests that those needs could include two elementary schools for the city school district, a middle school for the county school district, two senior centers, money for justice facilities and a community college, funds for parks and open space, and affordable housing initiatives.

How the pie is divided will be up to the task force to recommend, the commissioners to place on the ballot, and the voters to decide.

In 1992, county voters passed a $52 million bond referendum for school funding—$36 million for the city schools and $16 million for the county district. In 1993, a $5 million bond for farmland preservation and purchase of development rights failed.

In 1997, four out of five proposed bonds were approved. In a $60.6 million package, $47 million went for the schools, $6.1 million for parks, $1.8 million for affordable housing and $1.2 million for sewer expansion in Efland. A $4.6 million referendum to raise money for improvements to county buildings and senior centers failed.

In 1997, funds were allocated to build Smith Middle School, an addition to East Chapel Hill High, Pathways Elementary and half the cost of Cedar Ridge High School. Only the bond for Cedar Ridge High School has not been sold yet.

Money also was divvied up for renovations at six Orange County schools, four of the eight city elementaries, Philips Middle and Chapel Hill High.

Assistant County Manager Rod Visser said that $2.8 million of the $6.1 million bond for parks and open space has been sold to help fund projects. The $1.2 million for the Efland sewer project has not yet been spent and $700,000 of the $1.8 million for affordable housing has been committed to projects, Visser said.

—Excerpted with permission from
The Chapel Hill News,
March 14, 2001.

may go up while the government waits for funds to become available. While costs go up, the value of the dollar may go down due to inflation. Inflation helps the borrower, however. Because of inflation, the dollars the government pays back may be worth quite a bit less than the dollars the government borrowed several years earlier. Borrowing for capital projects also places responsibility for paying for the project on those who will use it. Capital projects have many years of useful life. Borrowing spreads out paying for the project over many of those years.

Governments borrow money by issuing **bonds.** Two kinds of bonds are used by North Carolina cities and counties. **General obligation** (G.O.) **bonds** pledge the "faith and credit" of the government. That is, the local government agrees to use tax money if necessary to repay the debt. Bondholders can even require local governments to raise taxes if that is necessary to pay the debt. **Revenue bonds** are repaid from revenues the project itself generates. Thus, if a parking deck is built with revenue bonds, the debt is repaid with revenues from fees paid by those who park there.

Under the North Carolina constitution, G.O. bonds cannot be issued unless a majority of the voters approve. A referendum must be held to allow voters to approve or reject all G.O. bonds proposed by city councils or boards of commissioners. G.O. bonds are typically used for non-revenue-producing projects like schools, courthouses, parks, or jails. Sometimes government officials also prefer to use G.O. bonds for revenue-producing projects like sewer plants, parking decks, or convention centers. This is because G.O. bonds usually have a lower **interest rate** than revenue bonds. Investors feel more secure about the repayment of their money when a bond is backed by local government's power to tax.

The **installment-purchase agreement** is an alternative to borrowing. Under this arrangement, someone else (a business or a civic group) builds or buys the facility the government needs. The government then gets to use the facility in return for an annual payment. Unlike rental agreements, however, in this kind of contract, the government is actually buying the property through its payments. Governments cannot pledge their taxing power when entering into installment-purchase agreements. The debt is backed by the property being purchased. If the government fails to complete its payments, the facility belongs to those who are leasing it to the government.

bond:
contract to repay borrowed money with interest at a specific time in the future

general obligation bond:
a loan that a government agrees to repay using tax money, even if the tax rate must be raised

revenue bond:
a loan that a government pays off with fees collected through operating the facility built with that loan

interest rate:
a percentage of the amount borrowed that the borrower agrees to pay to the lender as a charge for use of the lender's money

installment-purchase agreement:
an arrangement to buy something in which the buyer gets to use the item while paying for it in regularly scheduled payments

Orange County Bond Referendum Results, November 6, 2001 *(See "In the News..." p. 90)*

Purpose of Bond Order:	Bond Amount:	Votes in Favor:	Votes Against:
School Bonds	$47,000,000	11,868	8,179
Bonds for Parks, Recreation, and Open Space	$20,000,000	10,915	8,988
Bonds for Senior Centers	$4,000,000	10,762	9,080
Bonds for Low- and Moderate-Income Housing	$4,000,000	10,441	9,482

Revenues

Local governments get most of their money from taxes, user fees and charges, and funding from other governments. There are also several smaller revenue sources, including interest the government earns on its fund balance. The local economy and decisions of state and federal governments play a major part in local government funding. Local officials have only a few ways to increase the amount of revenue their local government receives.

Local Taxes

The **property tax** is the most important local tax. Property taxes are often the largest single source of revenue for a local government, sometimes providing more than half of all revenues. The property tax is based on the **assessed value** of property.

Assessing establishes the value of property for tax purposes. **Real property** must be reassessed every eight years, although some counties do so more often. **Personal property** (cars, trucks, business equipment) is reassessed each year. According to North Carolina law, tax assessments are supposed to be at the fair market value of the property. That is, the assessed value should equal the likely sale price of the property. If a property owner thinks an assessed value is too high, he or she may appeal it to the county commissioners when they meet as the "board of equalization and review."

Economic development increases the value of property in a city or county, thereby increasing its property **tax base.** New real estate developments are assessed as they are completed, so they immediately add to a jurisdiction's **total assessed value.** Unless there is new construction, however, real property is reassessed only every eight years in most counties. The market value of property may change a great deal during the eight years between reassessments.

The **property tax rate** is the amount of tax due for each $100 of assessed value. If a house and lot are valued at $100,000 and the property tax rate is $.90 per $100, the tax due on the property will be $900.

$$\frac{\$100,000}{\$100} = \$1,000 \qquad \$.90 \times 1,000 = \$900$$

The property tax is one of the few sources of revenue that the local governing board can influence directly. For this reason, setting the property tax rate is often the last part of budget review. To set the rate, local officials must first determine how much the city or county needs to raise in property taxes to balance the budget. All other estimated revenues are added together. That figure is subtracted from the total expenses the local government plans to have. The balance is the amount that must be raised through property taxes.

---

property tax:
a tax placed on the assessed value of land and property to be paid by the owner of that property

assessed value:
the value assigned to property by government to establish its worth for tax purposes

real property:
land and buildings, and improvements to either

personal property:
things people own other than land and buildings

tax base:
the value of the property, sales, or income being taxed

total assessed value:
the sum of the assessed value of all the property a city or county can tax

property tax rate:
a percentage of the assessed value of property that determines how much tax is due for that property

In the NEWS...

County Okays Tax Plan

By Johnny Whitfield

Mitchell County residents are getting closer to finding out how the county will value their land for tax purposes over the next eight years.

County commissioners gave their okay to preliminary assessments after tax assessor Mike Robinson gave the board a 90-minute presentation on how the values were [obtained].

The biggest bone of contention, Robinson said, will probably revolve around the assessments placed on values for land used in mining.

In prior revaluations, mining land was valued as timberland, but Robinson said state law allows local governments to value property based on the value of their mineral deposits and their status as land still to be mined.

According to Robinson, some of that land will increase in value from $1,200 per acre to more than $43,000 per acre.

"We've worked with the mining industries to determine what land is currently being mined and how they generate income from that land," Robinson said.

"We believe we could go to court and win a court case if it comes down to it," Robinson said.

With the formula for determining land values approved, residents have until February 5 to review the process before public hearing on the matter.

As for residential and commercial properties, Robinson said the tax office and Sabre Systems, the company hired to complete the revaluation, used a combination of market values and replacement costs to determine property values on those tracts of land.

The properties were also valued based, in part, on the neighborhood in which they are located.

Robinson said that was a necessary part of the process, because property in Buladean, for instance, doesn't bring as much in a sale as land in Swiss Pine Lake subdivision.

"You can look at any map of the sales that have taken place in the last two and a half or three years and tell that land values aren't the same," Robinson said.

Commissioners questioned Robinson on how neighborhoods were grouped and how land in the adjacent neighborhoods with differing characteristics was valued.

Robinson told commissioners that they were about to embark on one of the most dangerous political tasks they are assigned as commissioners.

"You will get more phone calls and more visits from people about this one issue than anything else you will be asked to do as commissioner," Robinson said.

—Excerpted with permission from
The Mitchell News-Journal,
January 23, 2001.

To set the property tax rate, the amount, which the government must raise through property taxes, is divided by the total assessed value of property in the jurisdiction. That gives the amount of tax that needs to be raised for each dollar of assessed value. To get the tax rate per $100 of assessed value, we multiply by 100. For example, if a city has a total assessed value of $500 million and needs to raise $4 million from property taxes, its property tax rate would be $.80 per $100 of assessed valuation.

$$\frac{\$4,000,000}{\$500,000,000} = .008 \qquad .008 \times \$100 = \$.80$$

The higher the assessed value of taxable property, the lower the tax rate needed to produce a given amount of revenue. If the assessed value of property in our last example were $600 million, the city could raise $4 million from property taxes with a property tax rate of only $.67 per $100 of assessed value.

The property tax rate for the next fiscal year is set by the local governing board when it adopts the annual budget. Sometimes there is considerable controversy over raising the property tax rate. Many people are quite aware of the property tax. Property owners get a bill from the local tax collector for the entire amount each

In the
NEWS...

Debts Due the City, Collection May Improve

By Terry Calhoun

Southport city manager Rob Gandy will ask aldermen to consider participating in a state debt collection program that deducts overdue municipal payments from N.C. Department of Revenue tax refund checks.

Gandy said the city only recently learned of the availability of the debt set-off program that legislators approved in 1997. The program enables cities and counties to match names of those in debt to the city with those who may be receiving state income tax refunds.

Brunswick County commissioners joined the state collection program last week. County manager Marty Lawing told commissioners they could expect roughly one-third of old accounts to be settled by the method.

Any and all debts of $50 or more owed the city—personal property, boat and vehicle taxes, water, sewer and electric utility charges and other fees charged by city departments—may be handled by the revenue department.

Gandy said he will review other requirements of the program before reporting to aldermen in January.

According to audited figures made available to aldermen earlier this month, Southport taxpayers owe the city $119,691—enough that, if all were paid today, city tax rates could be cut from the current 40 cents per $100 property valuation to 34 or 35 cents. Or, the money could be used for water and sewer improvements. Collection of delinquent water, sewer and electric payments could further benefit the city.

Alderman Paul Fisher repeatedly has encouraged city staff to more aggressively collect unpaid bills and has asked the city manager and city attorney to offer a plan to reduce the city's accounts receivable backlog.

Although back taxes may be collected for tax years reaching back a decade, $90,000 of the Southport debt is from tax years 1998–2000. Those figures are current as of the close of the fiscal year June 30, 2001, the latest audited numbers available.

The state set-off program might go far in satisfying Fisher that the city administration is doing all it can to collect owed taxes. Cumbersome and time-consuming mortgage lien procedures seldom produce immediate results.

Among other steps, the city would have to establish a hearing procedure and name a hearing officer and notify debtors by regular mail prior to turning the debt over to a clearinghouse.

Brunswick County is expected to contract with Five Star Computing of Columbia, S.C., for administration of the program and to act as the established clearinghouse.

—Reprinted with permission from
The State Port Pilot,
December 26, 2001.

year. Thus, people know exactly how much they pay in local property tax. (In contrast, the sales tax is collected a few pennies or a few dollars at a time. Most people lose track of how much they pay in sales tax.) Also, the connection between the property tax and the services government provides may be difficult to see. After all, people receive public services all year long, but the property tax bill comes only once a year.

Most property owners pay their taxes. In North Carolina, more than 95 percent of all property taxes are typically paid each year. When taxes on property are not paid, the government can go to court to take the property and have it sold to pay the tax bill.

Property tax bills are sent out in August, early in the new fiscal year, yet no penalties for late payment are imposed until January. Therefore, most people wait until December to pay their property taxes. Local governments must pay their bills each month. They cannot wait until they have received property tax payments to pay their employees and suppliers. This is another reason the fund balance is important. Local governments need to have money on hand to pay their bills while they wait for property taxes to be paid.

In addition to the property tax, some counties and cities have gotten authority from the General Assembly to levy certain other taxes. These include taxes for the privilege of doing business, keeping a dog or other pet, or owning an automobile. More than 70 counties and a few cities have authority to levy occupancy taxes on hotel and motel rooms. A smaller number of local governments have authority to levy a tax on the price of restaurant meals or on transfer of land. The General Assembly limits the amount of these taxes, usually to a few dollars each.

State-Collected Taxes

Sales tax provides a substantial part of most local governments' revenues. State law permits each county to levy a tax of $.02 on each dollar of sales in the county, and all the counties do so. (The state levies an additional $.045 on all sales except food. The county tax is applied to food. Mecklenburg County has special authority to levy an additional half-cent tax on sales in that jurisdiction.) Businesses collect the money from their customers at the time of sale. The state collects sales tax receipts from businesses throughout North Carolina and then returns the local portion of the sales tax to the counties and the municipalities within them.

Sales tax revenues are divided between county and municipal governments according to formulas established by the General Assembly. Each board of county commissioners decides whether sales tax revenues will be divided within that county's municipalities on the basis of a population formula or on the basis of the amount of taxes collected in each jurisdiction. City councils have

sales tax:
tax levied on a product at the time of sale

no control over how much sales tax revenue they receive, and county commissioners can only decide whether to divide sales tax receipts with cities either according to population or according to where the tax was paid. Only the state legislature can raise the sales tax rate. Neither city nor county officials have control over how much money the sales tax produces for local government.

Because the sales tax rate is set by the General Assembly, the amount of revenue in any year depends on economic conditions. The more people spend on purchases, the greater the sales tax revenue. When the economy slows down and people buy less, sales tax revenues go down too.

North Carolina has a separate tax on the sale of gasoline. A part of the state **gasoline tax** is distributed to each municipality in the state. This money, called **Powell Bill** funds, can be used only for the construction and maintenance of city streets. In FY 2001, more than $129 million dollars in Powell Bill funds were transferred from the state to cities and towns.

Because the gasoline tax is a tax on each gallon of gasoline purchased, when gasoline prices go up and people buy less gasoline, Powell Bill funds go down. This leaves cities with less money for streets.

gasoline tax:
a tax placed on purchases of gasoline

Powell Bill:
a North Carolina state law that allocates part of the state's gasoline tax to municipal governments to build and repair city streets

Cities and counties also receive money from the state for taxes on such things as sales of land, and beer and wine sales. The state also pays local governments money to replace some of the revenue lost when the state removed some property from the local tax base. Local officials have no control over these revenues, however. The General Assembly sets these tax rates and determines how the funds will be distributed.

User Fees

Local governments charge customers for many of the services they use. These charges are called "user fees." You pay a fee to swim at the public pool or play golf at the public park. You pay a fare to ride on the city bus. Cities and counties with public water supplies and sewer systems charge water and sewer customers based on the amount of water used. Some North

City and federal tax funds help subsidize bus service.

In the
NEWS...
Shelby's Sewer Rates Take a Hike

By Luann Laubscher

Residents will see a 10 percent increase in sewer rates on their February bills.

City Council voted Monday night to raise rates beginning Jan. 1, instead of immediately, to avoid customers receiving higher bills right after the holidays.

"I am reluctant to vote to raise rates," Mayor Mike Philbeck said, "but I see no other way."

City Manager Grant Goings said that the city staff has proposed more than $600,000 in budget cuts, but that alone will not solve the problem.

Council members were briefed last week about the state of the utility department's finances following the closing of two major water users, Shelby Dye and Finishing and Doran Mills. The closings created a loss of $322,000 in revenue, with more expected as the economy continues on a downslide.

Goings said he has been asked why the city can't work like a business and have lay-offs during times of financial trouble.

"The vast majority of our costs are fixed," Goings said. "That explains why—when we lose big users—we have to raise rates to recoup costs."

Goings said a third of the sewer budget is debt payments and that the workload at the water plant does not decrease.

"It stays consistent, regardless of the number of gallons of water we sell," he said.

Another reason the city cannot react like a business, Goings said, is because the city can't go out of business.

"By law we have to do what is necessary to provide a viable utility," Goings said. "We are not dealing with a profit margin."

Philbeck said he hoped the city would not have to go through with the other proposed sewer increases.

—Excerpted with permission from
The Shelby Star, December 3, 2001.

Carolina cities also operate the local electric service and charge customers for the electricity they use. These charges are all based on the cost of providing the service. The people who use these services help to pay for the direct benefits they get from them.

In many cases, the users do not pay the entire cost of providing the service, however. Governments **subsidize** services because the public also benefits from the service. For example, city bus fares are usually heavily subsidized because if people ride buses, fewer cars are on the streets. Bus riders help reduce traffic congestion and parking problems as well.

Local governing boards have the authority to set user fees. Next to the property tax, user fees are the largest source of local government revenue that local officials can control. As local governments have been asked to do more, local officials in many jurisdictions have begun to rely more on user fees to raise the necessary revenue. Fees for collecting solid waste have been established. Fees for building inspections and other regulation have also been increased to cover more of the costs of conducting these regulatory activities.

subsidize:
to reduce the amount users pay for a service by funding some of the cost from another source

Increased reliance on user fees means that more and more of the cost of public service is paid directly by the customer who gets the service. Less is paid as a **subsidy** from other sources, and so the cost for each user goes up. When the public has a great interest in seeing that everyone gets the service, regardless of ability to pay, user fees are kept low and taxpayers subsidize the cost of the service. User fees set at the full cost of service may mean that public benefits are lost. For example, if bus riders have to pay the full cost of buying and operating the buses, fares may be so high that most riders choose to have their own cars, adding to traffic congestion and the need for more street and parking construction.

subsidy:
a payment which reduces the cost to the user

State and Federal Aid

Local governments get some of their revenue from state and federal governments. Grants and other aid programs help local governments meet specific needs. During the 1960s and 1970s, **intergovernmental assistance** was a major source of local revenue. During the 1980s, many federal grant programs were abolished or greatly reduced and intergovernmental assistance became a much smaller part of local government revenues. Still, several important aid programs remain.

intergovernmental assistance:
money given to local governments by state and federal governments to help meet specific needs

Community Development Block Grants help cities and counties improve housing, public facilities, and economic opportunities in low-income areas. Projects funded under this federal program include installation of water and sewer lines, street paving, housing rehabilitation, and other community improvements.

Many social service benefits, such as Temporary Assistance to Needy Families, Medicaid, and food stamps are paid largely with federal funds. State grants also help to pay for some of the costs of social service programs. Local employees administer these programs. They determine who is eligible and see that appropriate benefits get to those who qualify. Counties also get some federal and state funds to help pay these administrative costs for social service programs, although most of the administrative costs must be paid from county funds.

State and federal funds are also provided to counties to support health and mental health services. A complex set of programs and regulations govern how these funds are used.

Other Local Revenues

assessment:
a charge imposed on property owners for building streets, sidewalks, water lines, sewers, or other improvements that government makes

When a city or county extends water and sewer lines to new areas, the owners of the property getting the new lines typically pay the local government a special **assessment.** The assessment helps cover the cost of constructing the new lines. Having public water supplies and sewer service available to the property increases its market value, so the owner is charged for the

Total Revenues for North Carolina's Municipalities: Fiscal Year 2000–2001

Total revenues: $7,206,419,619

Utility user fees: (33%) customers' payments for water and sewer services

Other user fees: (6%) fees for trash collections, inspections, and other services to customers

Property tax: (18%)

Sales tax: (8%)

Other governments: (13%) payments from federal, state, and other local governments; payments from the state of North Carolina comprise most of this amount

Debt proceeds: (11%) funds raised through borrowing

Other: (11%) interest earned on municipal fund balances, sale of municipal property, and other miscellaneous revenues

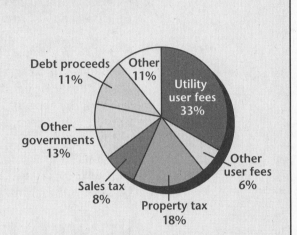

Source: North Carolina Department of the State Treasurer

Total Revenues for North Carolina's Counties: Fiscal Year 2000–2001

Total revenues: $9,671,338,222

Property tax: (35%)

Other taxes: (3%)

Sales tax: (12%)

User fees: (9%) fire protection charges, landfill charges, ambulance charges, cemetery charges, and all other services to customers for which fees are charged

Other governments: (24%)

Debt proceeds: (12%)

Other: (5%) licenses and permit charges, interest on county fund balances, and sale of county property

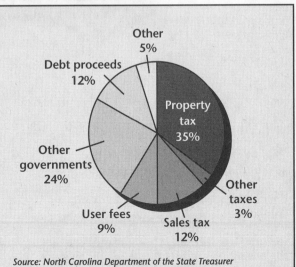

Source: North Carolina Department of the State Treasurer

improvement. Similarly, cities usually charge property owners along a street for paving the street or building sidewalks.

Interest earned on the fund balance can be another important revenue source. Most local governments try to maintain a fund balance equal to 15 to 20 percent of annual expenditures. This provides a ready source of funding for months when tax collections are slow. A sizable fund balance can also help cover an unexpected decrease in revenues. (Remember: local officials have little control over most of their revenues and cannot change the property tax rate they adopt with the annual budget.) Until the funds are needed, the fund balance can be invested and the interest added to government revenues.

For most municipalities, utility user fees are the biggest source of revenue. Property taxes are the county's largest source of revenue. The graphs on the previous page show the various sources for FY 2001 municipal and county revenues.

Report to the People

At the end of each fiscal year, every local government in North Carolina prepares an annual financial report. This document summarizes all of the government's financial activity: what it has received, what it has borrowed, what it has spent, what it is obligated to spend, and what it has in the fund balance. Each local government publishes its annual financial report, has it audited by an independent accounting firm, and files a financial summary with the Local Government Commission.

The report helps local officials better understand the financial situation of their government. The independent audit and the report to the Local Government Commission serve as checks on the accuracy of the report and the legality of the government's financial dealings. The publication of the report also informs citizens about their local government's financial condition.

Discussion Questions

1. Why is the annual budget important to each local government in North Carolina?

2. Why do local governments try to maintain a sizable fund balance?

3. How do user fees differ from taxes? What are the advantages of user fees as local government revenues? What are the disadvantages?

4. Acquire a copy of the annual budget for your county or city. How much did the county or city government spend and receive last year? How large was its fund balance?

5. What are the local property tax rates for your county and city? How much additional revenue would an increase of one cent in the property tax generate for each?

Making Government Work

8

Good government does not just happen. Good government is the result of people working together to decide what needs to be done for the community and then working to carry out those decisions. People make government work.

Who are the people involved in local government? This chapter explores the answer to that question. We consider six groups: voters, elected officials, local government employees, volunteers, members of appointed boards, and the general public.

People may be in several of these groups at once. For example, all voters are members of the general public, and all elected officials are also voters. Government employees may also be volunteers in other public agencies. They are almost always voters too. This chapter discusses the different groups separately to indicate the different ways people help shape the way government works.

Voters

The voters in each jurisdiction choose the members of their local governing boards. The voters in each county also elect a sheriff and a register of deeds. The voters must also approve any agreement by their local government to borrow money that will be repaid with tax receipts. Through voting, the people determine who their government leaders will be and give the officials they elect the authority to govern. Voting is, thus, the essential act of representative democracy. Voting is both a very special responsibility and a very important civil right.

Who can vote?

Struggles over the right to vote have continued ever since the United States gained independence from Great Britain. At independence, only free male citizens who were 21 years of age or older and paid taxes could vote for members of the lower house of the North Carolina General Assembly. Only men who met all these qualifications and also owned at least 50 acres of land could vote for members of the state senate. (There were no local elected officials.) Most African Americans were held as slaves and could not

Recent state legislation mandates elimination of punch card ballots by January 1, 2006. Here, an elections director tests an electronic voting system under consideration for use in her county.

vote at all. In 1835 the General Assembly prohibited even free men of African descent from voting in North Carolina.

The Civil War ended slavery, and in 1870 the Fifteenth Amendment to the United States Constitution extended voting rights to all male citizens 21 and older, regardless of "race, color, or previous condition of servitude." For the next few years, African Americans were able to vote as the Constitution permitted. In 1890 more than 1,000 black North Carolinians held office. But some white leaders feared an alliance between black voters and poor white voters. To prevent that alliance, some white leaders stirred up racial fears among whites and pushed racial segregation. The segregation laws were called "Jim Crow" laws. By the end of the nineteenth century, the North Carolina General Assembly had devised means of keeping most nonwhite men from voting, and the federal government refused to enforce the Constitution.

Women could not vote in North Carolina at the beginning of the twentieth century either, even though some people had long been seeking voting rights (or suffrage) for women. Finally, in 1920 the women's suffrage movement was successful. That year the Nineteenth Amendment to the United States Constitution extended the right to vote to female citizens 21 and older.

Although white women began to vote in North Carolina in the 1920s, most African American and Native American citizens of North Carolina were kept from voting until the 1960s. A major accomplishment of the civil rights movement, which also ended racial segregation in North Carolina, was the guarantee of voting rights for all adult citizens.

The last extension of voting rights came in 1971 when the Twenty-sixth Amendment to the United States Constitution guaranteed the right to vote to younger citizens. Now all citizens who are at least 18 years old are eligible to vote. Anyone who was born in the United States is a citizen. So are children born in other countries if either of their parents is a United States citizen. Other people who are born in other countries may become United States citizens through naturalization, a procedure administered by the U.S. State Department.

Being eligible to vote does not make you a voter, however. To be a voter, you must first register with the local board of elections in the county where you live. Seventeen-year-old citizens may register

In the NEWS...

A Sign of Citizenship

By Nathan Hall

The McDowell Board of Elections is making it easy for young people to register to vote this year. Staff members set up a sign-up booth at McDowell High Thursday afternoon during lunch periods. They said they were pleased with the turnout.

"We'd loved to have had more, but it was well worth the work and the time," said Elections Director Kim Welborn. "Hopefully we'll receive more by mail."

Forms were left in guidance office that students could mail in.

Both Welborn and elections assistant Cheryl Mitchell were there on behalf of the board helping students to register. At the end of the day, 65 students had filled out the forms. Currently, there are 304 seniors at McDowell High, and 17 at the Accelerated Learning Center. School officials said some juniors might also have been eligible to register.

The school announced the sign-up daily for about two weeks. Students were eligible to register if they were 18 or would be 18 before Nov. 5, 2003.

"Our record books will tell you that below the age of 25, there's just no participation," said Welborn. "We're going to change that."

Welborn said it was the first time the Board of Elections had visited the high school for registration sign-up.

Mitchell and Welborn said that they were going to the Accelerated Learning Center on Friday for registration sign-ups.

Welborn hopes that making registration convenient for students will increase the number of registered voters. Some students indicated that the relative easiness of the process was a motivation to sign up.

"I probably wouldn't have registered if it wasn't right here at school," said Bryan Gunter.

Students at McDowell High School register to vote.

But each student had a different reason for registering.

"It's important that I have a say in what goes on in this community," said Mila Wilmoth.

Avizia Long said she registered because she likes to keep up with current events.

Senior Lyric Thompson said she was glad to capitalize on the opportunity to vote once she turned 18. "I'm glad to express my opinion when given the opportunity," she said.

Senior Nicki Bradley said that she believes it is a privilege to get to pick who she wants to represent her.

"Voting is a good way to voice my opinions through other people," said Mandy Ledford.

The McDowell Board of Elections is also sponsoring a voting slogan contest for high school students. The winner will receive a basket containing free pizza coupons, free movie passes and rentals, free skating, bowling, ice cream and more. [Editor's note: Contest guidelines and details for submittal were included in the original article.]

—Excerpted with permission from
The McDowell News,
March 8, 2002.

ballot:
the list of candidates on
which you cast your vote

precinct:
a geographic area that contains a specific number of
voters

polling place:
an official place for voting

absentee ballot:
an official list of candidates
on which voters who can-
not get to the polling place
on election day indicate
their votes

if they will be eighteen years old by the next general election. Thus, you can register and vote in a primary election when you are seventeen if your eighteenth birthday comes before the November general election.

To vote, you must also cast your **ballot.** Each county is divided into voting **precincts.** The county board of elections establishes a place to vote—a **polling place**—in each precinct. Registered voters may cast their ballots in person at the polling place on Election Day. If they are unable to get to the polling place because of illness or travel, they may vote by **absentee ballot.**

People vote because they want to exercise their rights. They vote to support candidates, parties, or issues. They vote to oppose candidates, parties, or issues. They vote to make their communities better. They vote to show that the government belongs to them and because they feel responsible for helping to select public leaders.

Elected Officials

The elected leaders of local governments are the members of their governing boards. For counties, these are the county commissioners. For municipalities, they are the council members (or "aldermen" or commissioners) and mayor. These officials have the authority to adopt policies for local government and are responsible to the people for seeing that local government responds to public needs and works well to meet those needs.

The governing board is the local government's legislature. The members discuss and debate policy proposals. Under state law, the board has the authority to determine what local public services to provide, what community improvements to pursue, and what kinds of behavior and land use to regulate as harmful. The local governing board also sets local tax rates and user fees and adopts a budget for spending the local government's funds. The board appoints the manager who is chief administrator for the government. All of these are group decisions. The board votes, and a majority must approve any action.

Each local governing board has a presiding officer—someone who conducts the meetings of the governing board, speaks officially for the local government, and represents the government at ceremonies and celebrations. In cities and towns, this is the mayor. Voters elect the mayor in most North Carolina cities and towns. In a few of the state's municipalities, however, members of the local governing board elect a mayor from among the members of the board. The presiding officer for a county is the chairman of the board of county commissioners. In most North Carolina counties, the board elects one of its members as chairman. In one county, the voters elect the chairman of the board of county commissioners.

The sheriff and the register of deeds are elected to head their respective departments of county government. The sheriff's department operates the county jail; patrols and investigates crimes in areas of the county not served by other local police departments; and serves court orders and subpoenas. The register of deeds office maintains official records of land and of births, deaths, and marriages. Both the sheriff and the register of deeds hire their own staffs. They are not required to hire on the basis of merit, although their employees must meet basic requirements set by the state.

School board members are also local elected officials. School boards are like city and county governing boards, except their authority is more limited. They are responsible only for policies regarding the local public schools, and they cannot set tax rates or appropriate funds. The county commissioners determine how much money the county will spend to support local public schools.

All local elected officials represent the people of their jurisdiction. People often contact these elected officials to suggest policy changes or to express their opinions on policy proposals that are being considered by the board. Boards hold public hearings on particularly controversial issues to provide additional opportunities for people to tell the board their views on policy proposals.

Elected officials get their authority from the people. Campaigning for office gives candidates an opportunity to express their views about local issues and to hear what citizens want from their elected officials. Elections give voters the opportunity to choose candidates who share their views on issues. Through elections, voters give elected officials the authority to make decisions that everyone will have to obey. Through elections, voters also hold elected officials accountable. People can vote against an elected official who does not represent them and defeat that official in the next election.

ward: a section of a jurisdiction for voting, representative, or administrative purposes

Elections are held every two or four years, depending on the term of office established for each office. In jurisdictions where board members are elected by district or **ward,** each voter votes only for the candidate from his or her own district. In jurisdictions where members are elected at large, each voter may vote for as many candidates as there are positions to be filled. (Some jurisdictions have at-large

Mayors like Grady Spry of Cooleemee often speak for their local government in meetings with other public and private groups.

elections for board members, but require that candidates live in and run for seats representing specific districts.) Election by district may produce a more diverse governing board if minority groups are concentrated in some parts of the jurisdiction. Districts can be drawn around those population concentrations so that a group, which is a minority in the total population, is a majority within the district. Federal courts have required district elections in counties and municipalities that have substantial African American populations but have failed to elect African American board members.

Elections for county commissioners are held on the Tuesday after the first Monday in November in even-numbered years, along with elections for state officials and members of Congress. The county sheriff and register of deeds are elected then too. In practice, the sheriff and register of deeds are often reelected, term after term. Often sheriffs and registers of deeds serve until they choose to retire. Frequently their successors have served as their deputies. Sometimes, however, these elections are highly contested—especially the elections for sheriff.

partisan:
involving political parties

political party:
an association of voters with broad common interests who want to influence or control decision making in government by electing the party's candidates to public office

County elections are **partisan.** That is, candidates run under **political party** labels. Primary elections are held several months before the November general election. Primary elections are elections among the candidates of a party to choose the party's candidates for the general election. In the primary election, members of each party vote only for their party's candidate. The two major political parties are the Democratic Party and the Republican Party. Other parties and non-party candidates may also be placed on the ballot by filing petitions.

Elections for city council members (or aldermen) are held in odd-numbered years. Election for mayor is held at the same time in those cities and towns where the voters elect the mayor. Most cities and towns have nonpartisan elections. That is, candidates do not run under party labels. These municipalities may have local voters' organizations that support candidates, but the Democratic and Republican parties are not permitted to run candidates in most North Carolina municipalities. Only a few cities and towns hold primary elections.

Campaign signs line a busy road in Oak Island just before the 2001 municipal elections.

Working for Local Government

Mission Accomplished

By Richard Nubel

Presiding over her final meeting as top elected official of the Town of Oak Island Tuesday night, Mayor Joan P. Altman gaveled to a close a remarkable decade-long term of service to her town. By week's end, a moving van will pull up to the SE 27th Street home she and her husband, Bruce, have occupied for the last 17 years and former mayor Altman's transition to citizen Joan Altman of Rockford, Ill., will have begun in earnest.

Behind, she leaves a legacy few who have served local government have matched. She leaves a town dramatically changed from that which existed in the first days of her service in 1991.

Most significantly, Altman leaves an office—the office of mayor—on which she has indelibly left her mark. As mayor of Long Beach until 1999 and of Oak Island until this week, she has recast the position of mayor, transforming it from once-monthly moderator and cutter of ribbons to a statewide and national spokesman for the town and all of its individual interests.

In her unique public service career, Altman was unwilling to sit only at the head of town government's table. She took the causes of Long Beach and Oak Island to the halls of the state's General Assembly and to Capitol Hill. She has testified before sessions of the state House and has served on legislative study commissions and special investigative bodies for regulatory agencies.

Her talents as a lobbyist on behalf of Long Beach and Oak Island led her to co-found a statewide advocacy group for coastal local government, the N.C. Beach and Shore Preservation Association, and to become its first executive director. Whether the issue was transportation, infrastructure, beach nourishment or protection of the environment, Altman was Oak Island's point person, representing it to its municipal neighbors, to Brunswick County, to North Carolina and to the nation.

Mayor Joan P. Altman

At home she led the town as it firmly set out its land use preferences and sought to provide the infrastructure that would support them. With the late Dot Kelly, mayor of Yaupon Beach, Altman gently but skillfully facilitated the consolidation of two island towns into one and then completed annexation of mainland tracts to the resulting new town.

"The thing I'm proudest of is being able to provide the working environment for town council so it can do its job," Altman said. "We've been able to do that by developing a cooperative relationship with staff, then encouraging council members to share their differences and to work together on those issues where consensus exists. A lot of times issues die because people won't spend the time trying to find consensus. I knew that was the mayor's role—to build consensus."

"Sand on the beach, consolidation—it took council and staff," Altman said. "I couldn't have done these things by myself. Council said these things are important. I just put in the time to make it happen."

She leaves big shoes for her successor to fill. "The mayor is going to have to continue to be a strong advocate for the town, as well as handling the day-to-day responsibilities," Altman said. "There aren't many jobs you can take and truly make them

(Continued from page 107)

your own. The mayor's job is one."

Oak Island's charter says only that the mayor will preside over monthly meetings of town council and will serve as head of town government, but the scope of the mayor's job is unlimited, Altman believes. "If you look at attending meetings and cutting ribbons, then doing the mayor's job isn't much," Altman said. "But if you look at the possibilities, then it becomes very personal, because everyone will look at it differently. The mayor's job is defined by the talents and skills of the person in that position and the time he gives to it. So, it is always going to be a very personalized job."

"One of the reasons I ran for office was because I wanted to raise people's expectations for what their government could be and what it can do," Altman said. "And that, is really it."

Mission accomplished.

—Excerpted with permission from *The State Port Pilot,* September 12, 2001.

Most school board elections are also nonpartisan. School board elections are in even-numbered years, with some at the time of the general election, some at the time of the primary election, and some on special election dates.

Altogether, more than 700 elected officials serve the state's county governments and 3,000 elected officials serve in North Carolina municipalities.

Why do people run for a seat on the local governing board? They may be interested in getting local government to adopt a particular policy proposal. They may want to help shape the future of the community more generally. They may feel an obligation to serve the public. They may want to explore politics and perhaps prepare for seeking state or federal office. They may enjoy exercising public responsibility or being recognized as a public leader.

Local Government Employees

Counties and municipalities hire many different kinds of workers. Counties hire nurses, social workers, sanitation inspectors, librarians, and many other specialists to perform county services. Similarly, cities hire police officers, engineers, machinery operators, recreation supervisors, and a wide variety of other specialists to carry out their services. In addition, both city and county governments hire accountants, clerks, maintenance workers, secretaries, administrators, and other staff to support the work of the government. These employees organize government activities; keep government records and accounts of public money; clean and repair government property; and pay the government's bills.

North Carolina local governments employed over 130,000 people in 1999. Local governments thus employed, on average, about 17 people for every 1,000 residents of the state.

Most North Carolina local governments have well-established systems for hiring employees on the basis of their qualifications for the job. In some other states, people who work for local government get their jobs because of personal or political connections. Hiring based on kinship is called **nepotism,** hiring based on friendship is called **favoritism,** and hiring based on political support is called **patronage.** Most North Carolina local governments have and enforce rules against nepotism, favoritism, and patronage. Instead, local governments in North Carolina usually hire people who have the training and experience to do the job they are being hired for. This is known as hiring based on **merit.** Local governments in North Carolina hire people on the basis of merit because their primary concern is having employees who can provide the best government services for the lowest cost. In a merit system, people are also promoted or dismissed on the basis of their job performance, rather than for personal or political reasons.

Except in the smallest North Carolina local governments, the governing board appoints a manager who is responsible for hiring, promoting, and dismissing government employees. The board judges the manager on how well services are provided and how well government funds are used. Thus, the manager wants to be sure that employees are doing their jobs well.

In larger counties and cities, the manager assigns much of the work of hiring and supporting the government's employees to a human resources (or personnel) department. To guide its work, the human resources department prepares job descriptions for all employees.

nepotism:
hiring or giving favorable treatment to someone based on kinship

favoritism:
showing partiality; favoring someone over others

patronage:
hiring or giving favorable treatment to an employee because he or she is a member of one's political party

merit:
hiring or promoting based on a person's qualifications, ability, and performance

Firefighters are among the many local government employees serving the people of North Carolina.

An employee's job description lists the duties of the job. When a job becomes vacant, the local government uses the job description to advertise the position. The personnel department accepts job applications from people who would like to be hired for the vacant position. In filling out the job application, the applicant lists his or her education, job training, skills, and previous work experience. The personnel department reviews the applications and selects the applicants who appear to be best qualified for the job. Applicants are often asked to provide the names of **references.** References are often asked about the applicant's performance or work ethic. The final set of applicants is then selected and interviewed, usually by the person who would supervise their work if they were hired. That person is usually responsible for recommending who gets hired.

references:
people who know how well someone did on a previous job or about that person's other qualifications for a job

Most local government employees enjoy their jobs and working for the public. They are honest, hard-working people who care about making their community a better place.

Volunteers

Volunteers also help carry out important public services. In many places in North Carolina, volunteers fight fires and provide emergency rescue services. Volunteers assist in programs for young persons, the elderly, homeless persons, and other groups with special needs. The volunteers may be organized through a city or county's fire department, recreation department, social services department, or other division of government. The volunteers may also be organized through a nonprofit corporation that works in cooperation with local government.

Like their full-time, paid counterparts, volunteer firefighters and emergency medical service technicians are required to have extensive training. In fact, most of the unincorporated areas of the state and most of the small municipalities depend on volunteers for fire fighting. Also, many counties rely on volunteer emergency rescue squads to provide medical assistance and rescue work.

Many volunteer fire departments are organized as nonprofit corporations. They have contracts with a local government to provide fire protection to a specific area. The volunteer fire department receives public funds to buy equipment and supplies needed in fighting fires. Similarly, municipal and county governments often provide buildings or funding for emergency shelters, senior citizens centers, hot lunch programs, youth recreation leagues, and other services operated by nonprofit organizations and staffed by volunteers.

Members of Appointed Boards

Local governments also have appointed boards or commissions. These provide opportunities for many other citizens to assist the elected governing board in shaping public policy. State law requires that some of these (such as Alcoholic Beverage Control boards, and boards of elections, health, mental health, and social services) play a direct role in selecting agency heads and setting operating policies for the agency. Other boards are established by the local government to provide policy direction for airports, civic centers, public housing, stadiums, or other public facilities. Still other boards advise elected officials directly on matters ranging from the environment to human relations, from recreation to job training, from open space to transportation. Large cities and counties may have more than 30 appointed boards and commissions, and many hundreds of citizens may serve on the boards of a large local government.

In many cases, at least some of the members of an appointed board must be selected from specific groups in the community. For example, a mental health board must include, among others, a physician, an attorney, and a "primary consumer in recovery and representing the interests of individuals with drug abuse." Other boards and commissions may require that members be residents of various parts of the jurisdiction to provide broad geographic representation. County boards of elections must include both Democrats and Republicans, with the party of the governor having the majority of members.

A volunteer takes part in an Earth Day creek cleanup to help improve his community.

People volunteer to serve on appointed boards and commissions for many of the same reasons people run for election. Having a particular concern for the subject the board deals with is especially important for many volunteers. Appointed boards have a narrower range of concerns than city councils or county commissions. Appointed boards provide an opportunity for people with a particular interest in historic preservation, nursing homes, or other public policy area to work on policy for that particular concern.

The General Public

Everyone uses local government services, is affected by the decisions local government makes, and influences local government decisions. Sometimes people are not aware of how they are

Wake Planners, Commissioners Seek to Define Responsibilities

By Bonnie Rochman

On Monday morning, accusations rebounded off the walls of a Wake County conference room.

We're underappreciated, one side said.

We don't understand why you make some of the decisions you do, said the other side.

Though it had the overtones of a marriage counseling session, it wasn't. Instead, it was a much needed tête-à-tête between the Wake County planning board and the county commissioners.

The two boards—the latter elected, the former appointed by them—rarely meet. In fact, officials find it hard to recall the last time they convened.

They're frustrated because despite the lack of communication, they are supposed to work together harmoniously and toward the same cause. Only until Monday, no one was quite sure what that cause was.

After batting around theories of who's responsible for what, commissioners and planning board members agreed that the planning board should serve as a lightning rod for "whatever is on the cutting edge of planning," as commissioner Betty Mangum summarized.

"Part of the role of the planning board is to anticipate, to read the environment, to get out front on an issue," planning board member Dwight Pearson said.

It's a crucial task because Wake County's future hinges on how the rest of the county is developed. That's where the members of the planning board come in. It's their job to examine development proposals and make recommendations to the commissioners.

Commissioners aren't bound to follow the planning board's advice, but they often do. Of course, other concerns sometimes enter the picture. Michael Weeks, chairman of the commissioners, said the "political reality" means "sometimes there are issues that are going to be difficult to deal with," and as a result the commissioners vote contrary to the planning board's recommendations.

A pressing issue facing both boards is the ongoing debate about land use, or what kinds of development should go where as Wake continues its transition from rural to urban, and its population grows from about 600,000 now to a projected 940,000 in 20 years. The county makes decisions about areas outside the jurisdiction of Wake's 12 municipalities.

Rather than waiting for developers to present proposals to the county, the boards said the county should take a more proactive role. How they might do that is unclear but important to figure out in coming sessions between the two boards.

"We want Wake County to be a place where people want to live," said Planning Director Mike Jennings.

—Reprinted with permission from *The News & Observer,* Raleigh, North Carolina, January 30, 2001.

influencing public policy. Other times they might be trying very hard to change local government policies. People unintentionally influence local government policies through the use of government services, cooperation (or noncooperation) with government programs, and through public behavior that harms others.

How does using government services affect public policy? Government officials often consider use to indicate the public's wants or needs. According to this view, the more people use a service, the more of that service the government should try to provide.

Local governments may sometimes be unable to provide more of a service, or officials may decide they cannot afford to do so. In such a situation, officials may try to limit use, but limiting use is also a government policy.

For example, the more often people use a ball field, the fewer hours it is available for other users. Government officials might respond to this increase in use by putting up lights so the field could also be used at night. They might also build additional fields so that more teams could play at the same time. These are examples of adding more service in response to increased use. But the local governing board might decide it could not afford to add lights or new fields. Instead, officials might decide to limit use of the existing field. They might require people who want to use the field to reserve it in advance, pay a fee, or join a league that schedules games on the field. These are all ways of rationing the service.

Cooperating or failing to cooperate with government programs also influences public policy in important ways. Many programs can succeed only if people cooperate. Consider the problem of solid waste disposal, for example. Many local governments have recycling programs to reduce the amount of waste that goes into landfills. Most of these recycling programs depend on people sorting their own trash so that recyclable materials can be collected separately from waste for the landfill. If people do sort their trash, the program succeeds. If they do not, the program will not work, and officials will have to find other ways to get rid of the trash people produce.

Behavior that harms people helps shape public policy because it creates a problem that local government attempts to reduce through regulation. When some people in a community indicate that they are offended, annoyed, or hurt by others' actions, local officials have to respond. The officials may decide that the action is so harmful that it should be regulated, or they may decide that the action is not causing enough of a problem to justify regulation.

Influencing Public Policy

Talking directly to public officials is one very important way to influence policy. People can call officials or visit them in person to discuss problems they think require government attention. They may also speak at public hearings or other meetings attended by public officials. Letters to public officials or petitions signed by large numbers of people are also ways people communicate their views about what government should do.

Often it is important to organize public support for a proposal. Officials are frequently persuaded by the reasons people provide in arguing for or against a proposal, but they can also be persuaded when large numbers of people agree. To organize support, people publicize the problem and the response they think government should make. They may hold news conferences or demonstrations to get the attention of newspapers, radio, and television. They may also write letters to the editor.

People can and do seek to use government for their own personal purposes. But many people are also interested in helping make the entire community a better place to live and work. People may disagree about whether a particular proposal is in the public interest, and debate is important. It is important to ask how the community would improve and this helps focus attention on the public benefits of government action. People who want the government to act should be able to explain how they think the proposed action will help improve conditions generally.

Good government depends on the public being aware of the problems and opportunities facing the community. Good government requires that many people learn about public issues and try to influence public policy. Good government requires that people register to vote and then actually do so. Good government requires that many people volunteer to help government, including running for elective office. Good government requires that well-qualified people make full-time careers serving as employees of local government. Good government will increasingly depend on you, as you become an adult in your community.

Discussion Questions

1. Who do you know who are local government employees? Who do you know who volunteers for local government work? Who do you know who has been elected to local office? Who do you know who serves on appointed boards?

2. What was the most recent local election in your city or county? How many people voted? How many people are registered to vote in your city or county? What was the voter turnout in the most recent election? (That is, what percentage of the registered voters voted in that election?) Are elections in your city or county by district or at large? How does that affect representation in your local government?

3. How have you or your family, friends, or neighbors been involved in influencing local government decisions?

4. Newspaper articles and radio and television newscasts often mention disagreements over whether or not local government should regulate certain behavior. Identify a local government law or regulation that has been the subject of disagreement where you live.

Which government regulation is involved?

What activities does the law or regulation apply to?

What are the arguments in favor of this government regulation?
   Hint: Who might be harmed without the regulation?
   How might they be harmed?

What are the arguments against this government regulation?
   Hint: Who might be harmed by the regulation?
   How might they be harmed?

If you had to decide whether or not to pass this law or regulation, what would you decide to do? Why?

For Further Reading

Books

Bell, A. Fleming II, Ed., *County Government in North Carolina*, 4th ed., Institute of Government, University of North Carolina at Chapel Hill, NC, 1999. Written for county officials to use as a reference, this book includes information about administering county government, elections, property taxes, and social services.

The Big Click: Photographs of One Day in North Carolina, April 21, 1989, Mobility, Inc., Richmond, VA, 1989. This collection of color photographs taken by numerous photographers shows different activities that people in North Carolina undertake at similar times in a single day.

Bledsoe, Jerry, *Carolina Curiosities—Jerry Bledsoe's Outlandish Guide to the Dadblamedest Things to See and Do in North Carolina,* Fast and McMillan Publishers, Inc., Charlotte, NC, 1984. This funny guidebook of places to see and things to do in North Carolina includes the site of Babe Ruth's first home run, Hog Day, the home of the man with the world's strongest teeth, and other oddities.

Coates, Albert, *The People and Their Government,* self-published, 1977. A discussion of citizen participation in local government identifies volunteer positions in local governments.

Corbitt, David Leroy, *The Formation of the North Carolina Counties, 1663–1943,* State Department of Archives, Raleigh, NC, 1969. This history of North Carolina counties includes how they evolved and how their geographical boundaries have changed.

Couch, Ernie and Jill Couch, *North Carolina Trivia,* Rutledge Hill Press, Nashville, TN, 1986. This fun trivia book about North Carolina includes questions on geography, history, sports, and science.

Crutchfield, James, *The North Carolina Almanac and Book of Facts,* Rutledge Hill Press, Nashville, TN, 1988. This extensive collection of facts about North Carolina discusses prominent North Carolinians and the history of the state.

Fleer, Jack, D., *North Carolina Government and Politics,* University of Nebraska Press, Lincoln, NE, 1994. This overview of state government and politics examines the context of local government in North Carolina.

Gade, Ole and H. Daniel Stillwell, *North Carolina: People and Environment,* Geo-APP, Boone, NC, 1986. This compilation of geographical information and other data about cities, counties, and rural areas in North Carolina includes predictions about the future of each region.

Grey, Gibson, Ed., *Community Problems and Opportunities in North Carolina,* self-published, Lumberton, NC, 1989.

Jones, H.G., *North Carolina Illustrated 1524–1984,* University of North Carolina Press, Chapel Hill, NC, 1983. This book is an extensive collection of historical photos from North Carolina with explanations of the significance of each photo.

Lawrence, David and Warren J. Wicker, Ed., 2nd ed., *Municipal Government in North Carolina,* Institute of Government, University of North Carolina at Chapel Hill, Chapel Hill, NC, 1996. Written as a reference for city officials, this book includes the history, roles and forms of municipal government in North Carolina, and sections on environmental affairs, community development, budgeting, and law enforcement.

Luebke, Paul, *Tarheel Politics: Myths and Realities,* University of North Carolina Press, Chapel Hill, NC, 1990. This discussion of politics in North Carolina describes conflicts between the "modernizers," who want to transform the state and the "traditionalists," who feel that change is unnecessary.

Luebke, Paul, *Tarheel Politics 2000,* University of North Carolina Press, Chapel Hill, NC, 1998. This is a revised and updated version of Luebke's earlier *Tarheel Politics: Myths and Realities.* The author is a college professor who also serves as a representative in the North Carolina General Assembly.

Massengill, Steven and Robert Topkins, *A North Carolina Postcard Album, 1905–1925,* Division of Archives and History, North Carolina Department of Cultural Resources, Raleigh, NC, 1988. This collection of picture postcards depicts North Carolina people and scenes in the early years of this century.

Orr, Douglas M., Jr., and Alfred W. Stuart, *The North Carolina Atlas,* University of North Carolina Press, Chapel Hill, NC, 2000. This collection of maps, pictures, and articles includes information about North Carolina's land, people, economy, government, and society. It also contains considerable details about the state's counties and municipalities.

Powell, William S., *Dictionary of North Carolina Biographies,* University of North Carolina Press, Chapel Hill, NC, 1979. This four-volume set of biographies includes prominent North Carolina citizens who have made a difference in the state.

Powell, William S., *North Carolina: A Bicentennial History,* Norton, New York, NY, 1977. This history of North Carolina from the colonial period to the 1970s gives readers a thorough background of the state.

Powell, William S., *The North Carolina Gazetteer,* University of North Carolina Press, Chapel Hill, NC, 1968. This geographical dictionary of North Carolina discusses how land formations, lakes, mountains, rivers, towns, and counties in the state were named.

Schumann, Marguerite, *The Living Land: An Outdoor Guide to North Carolina,* Dale Press of Chapel Hill, Chapel Hill, NC, 1977. This guide to natural resources in North Carolina includes listings of lakes, forests, mountains, and beaches that are accessible to the public.

Periodicals

County Lines, Raleigh, NC: North Carolina Association of County Commissioners. This newsletter discusses information and issues about counties in North Carolina and the people who work for those counties.

NC Insight, Raleigh, NC: North Carolina Center for Public Policy Research. Written by the North Carolina Center for Public Policy Research, this journal presents North Carolina policy issues and makes recommendations for improving public policies.

North Carolina Historical Review, Raleigh, NC: North Carolina Historical Commission. This compilation of articles about the history of North Carolina includes important people, events, and anecdotes.

Popular Government, Chapel Hill, NC: University of North Carolina Institute of Government. This journal contains articles about North Carolina government and current concerns of its citizens.

Southern Cities, Raleigh, NC: North Carolina League of Municipalities. This newsletter includes stories about the people in city and town government, issues facing municipal government, and innovative programs for dealing with these problems.

Web Sites

http://ncinfo.iog.unc.edu/ is the Web site of the Institute of Government at the University of North Carolina at Chapel Hill. This site provides access to North Carolina local governments' Web sites and to the Web sites of newspapers throughout the state, as well as to the publications, resources, and programs of the Institute of Government.

www.civics.org is the Web site of the North Carolina Civic Education Consortium. This site provides access to resources for teaching and learning about government and public policy in North Carolina and other states.

www.ncgov.com is the official Web site of the state of North Carolina. This site provides access to both official state agencies and to many other sources of information about government and public policy in North Carolina.

absentee ballot: an official list of candidates on which voters who cannot get to the polling place on election day indicate their votes (p. 103)

allocate: to set aside money for a specific purpose (p. 33)

annexation: the legal process of extending municipal boundaries and adding territory to a city or town (p. 16)

appropriate: to assign government funds to a particular purpose or use (p. 88)

assessed value: the value assigned to property by government to establish its worth for tax purposes (p. 92)

assessment: a charge imposed on property owners for building streets, sidewalks, water lines, sewers, or other improvements that government makes (p. 98)

ballot: the list of candidates on which you cast your vote (p. 103)

bond: contract to repay borrowed money with interest at a specific time in the future (p. 91)

business development corporation: a group of people legally organized as a corporation to encourage economic development (p. 61)

capital: previously manufactured goods used to make other goods and services; local governments' capital includes land, buildings, equipment, water and sewer lines, city streets and bridges (p. 89)

chamber of commerce: a group of business people formed to promote business interests in the community (p. 61)

charter: the document defining how a city or town is to be governed and giving it legal authority to act as a local government (p. 16)

citation: an official summons to appear before a court to answer a charge of violating a government regulation (p. 84)

civil: concerns government's role in relations among citizens (p. 84)

coastal plain: the eastern region of North Carolina, extending approximately 150 miles inland from the coast. The western border of the region is usually defined as the western boundaries of Northhampton, Halifax, Nash, Johnston, Harnett, Hoke, and Scotland counties; includes 41 counties (p. 25)

compost: decayed material that is used as fertilizer (p. 48)

contract: an agreement made between two or more people or organizations (p. 16)

corporation: a group of persons formed by law to act as a single body (p. 16)

council-manager plan: an arrangement for local government in which the elected legislature hires a professional executive to direct government activities (p. 19)

crime: an act that is forbidden by law; an offense against all of the people of the state, not just the victim of the act (p. 70)

debt service: payments of principal and interest on a loan (p. 89)

desalinization: the process by which the salt is taken out of sea water (p. 43)

developer: a person or business that builds houses or prepares land for building (p. 80)

dispatcher: a person who gives emergency workers information so that those workers can respond to emergencies (p. 54)

economic development: activities to create new jobs and additional sales and other business (p. 57)

expenditures: money spent (pp. 33, 86)

extraterritorial land use planning jurisdiction: the area outside city limits over which a city has authority for planning and regulating use (p. 76)

favoritism: showing partiality; favoring someone over others (p. 109)

federal system: the sharing of power between the central and state governments (p. 2)

fiscal year: the 12-month period that may not coincide with the calendar year used by the government for record keeping, budgeting, taxing, and other aspects of financial management (p. 86)

food stamps: a program to help people with financial need buy food; vouchers to be used like money for purchasing food; federal program, but administered by county departments of social services in North Carolina (p. 34)

fund balance: money a government has not spent at the end of the year (p. 86)

gasoline tax: a tax placed on purchases of gasoline (p. 96)

general obligation bond: a loan that a government agrees to repay using tax money, even if the tax rate must be raised (p. 91)

grant: money given by state or federal government to local governments to fund local projects (p. 4)

greenspace: an area that is kept undeveloped to provide more open land in or near a city (p. 79)

ground water: water that collects underground (p. 42)

impurities: materials that pollute (p. 43)

incident report: a report that a police officer writes describing a crime or other problem situation (p. 54)

incineration: the safe burning of wastes (p. 51)

incorporate: to receive a state charter, officially recognizing the government of a locality (p. 16)

initiative: a way in which the citizens propose laws by gathering voter signatures on a petition; only a few cities and no counties in North Carolina have provisions for this (p. 73)

installment-purchase agreement: an arrangement to buy something in which the buyer gets to use the item while paying for it in regularly scheduled payments (p. 91)

interest: a charge for borrowed money that the borrower agrees to pay the lender (p. 89)

interest rate: a percentage of the amount borrowed that the borrower agrees to pay to the lender as a charge for use of the lender's money (p. 91)

intergovernmental assistance: money given to local governments by state and federal governments to help meet specific needs (p. 98)

jurisdiction: the right to use legal authority or the territory over which a government can use its authority (p. 2)

levy: to impose a tax by law (p. 16)

liability: something for which one is obligated according to law (p. 16)

local act: a state law that applies to only one local government (p. 18)

mandate: a legal order by which one government requires actions by another government (p. 4)

mandated service: a program which local governments must provide because of requirements from state or federal government (p. 23)

Medicaid: a program designed to pay for medical care for people in financial need; federal program, but administered by county departments of social services in North Carolina (p. 34)

merit: hiring or promoting based on a person's qualifications, ability, and performance (p. 109)

mountain counties: the western region of North Carolina, extending eastward from the Tennessee border to the eastern boundaries of Alleghany, Wilkes, Caldwell, Burke, and Rutherford counties; includes 23 counties (p. 25)

mulch: material spread around plants that prevents the growth of weeds and protects the soil from drying out (p. 48)

municipality: a city, town, or village that has an organized government with authority to make laws, provide services, and collect and spend taxes and other public funds (p. 2)

mutual aid agreement: commitments by local governments to assist each other in times of need (p. 5)

nepotism: hiring or giving favorable treatment to someone based on kinship (p. 109)

opponent: one who is against something (p. 69)

optional service: a program that a government decides to provide to meet the needs or requests of its residents (p. 24)

ordinance: a law, usually of a city or county (p. 17)

partisan: involving political parties (p. 106)

patronage: hiring or giving favorable treatment to an employee because he or she is a member of one's political party (p. 109)

per capita: equally to each person; by or for each person (p. 30)

personal property: things people own other than land and buildings (p. 92)

personnel: the people who work for a government, company, or other organization (p. 20)

petition: a request for government action signed by a number of voters who support the same request (p. 69)

piedmont: the central region of North Carolina including Surry, Yadkin, Alexander, Catawba, and Cleveland counties on the west, and Warren, Franklin, Wake, Chatham, Lee, Moore, and Richmond counties on the east; includes 36 counties (p. 26)

political party: an association of voters with broad common interests who want to influence or control decision making in government by electing the party's candidates to public office (p. 106)

poll tax: tax people had to pay in order to be allowed to vote (p. 65)

polling place: an official place for voting (p. 103)

Powell Bill: a North Carolina state law that allocates part of the state's gasoline tax to municipal governments to build and repair city streets (p. 96)

precinct: a geographic area that contains a specific number of voters (p. 103)

principal: the amount of money borrowed (p. 89)

privatization: government buying a service from a business instead of producing the service itself (p. 40)

property tax: a tax placed on the assessed value of land and property to be paid by the owner of that property (p. 92)

property tax rate: a percentage of the assessed value of property that determines how much tax is due for that property (p. 92)

proponent: one who is in favor of something (p. 69)

proposal: a suggestion put forward for consideration or approval (p. 68)

real property: land and buildings, and improvements to either (p. 92)

references: people who know how well someone did on a previous job or about that person's other qualifications for a job (p. 110)

referendum: a way for citizens to vote on state or local laws (p. 8); an election in which citizens vote directly on a public policy question (p. 73)

regional council: an organization of local governments established to deal with mutual challenges; 17 exist in North Carolina (p. 5)

revenue: the income that a government collects for public use (p. 85)

revenue bond: a loan that a government pays off with fees collected through operating the facility built with that loan (p. 91)

rural: of or relating to the country; area where fewer people live (p. 25)

sales tax: tax levied on a product at the time of sale (p. 95)

septic tank: a container in which wastes are broken down by bacteria (p. 44)

sludge: the solid material separated from sewage (p. 46)

subdivision regulation: rules for dividing land for development (p. 76)

subsidize: to reduce the amount users pay for a service by funding some of the cost from another source (p. 97)

subsidy: a payment which reduces the cost to the user (p. 98)

sue: to ask a court to act against a person or organization to prevent or pay for damage by that person or organization (p. 16)

surface water: all waters on the surface of the Earth found in rivers, streams, lakes, ponds, and so on (p. 43)

tax base: the value of the property, sales, or income being taxed (p. 92)

Temporary Assistance to Needy Families (TANF): federal government program of support for families in need; provides small payments to cover basic living expenses and assistance to help adults find and keep jobs (p. 36)

total assessed value: the sum of the assessed value of all the property a city or county can tax (p. 92)

unincorporated: the part of a county outside the cities and towns in that county (p. 24)

urban: area where people live close together; most incorporated as municipalities (p. 25)

variance: permission to do something different from what is allowed by current regulations (p. 77)

volunteers: people who donate their time and effort (p. 61)

ward: a section of a jurisdiction for voting, representative, or administrative purposes (p. 105)

watershed: an area that drains water into a stream or lake (p. 43)

zoning: rules designating different areas of land for different uses (p. 76)